GET UP!

GET UP!

God's Children Don't Beg

D. Steve Walker

GET UP!
GOD'S CHILDREN DON'T BEG

iUniverse books may be ordered through booksellers or by contacting:

iUniverse
1663 Liberty Drive
Bloomington, IN 47403
www.iuniverse.com
844-349-9409

ISBN: 978-1-6632-4180-1 (sc)
ISBN: 978-1-6632-4181-8 (hc)
ISBN: 978-1-6632-4182-5 (e)

Library of Congress Control Number: 2022912293

Print information available on the last page.

iUniverse rev. date: 07/27/2022

Contents

Preface

Is Your Coffee Really Black?

There's an interesting thing about black coffee that intrigues me. Coffee Beans never actually become black, although brewed coffee may 'look' black. People, based on their actions, can seem that way as well.

A lot of people of color may 'look' like us but are not 'good' for us—those who feel they are "blessed" to do what God calls a *mess*. Many have gained much success entertaining us with their bad habits for the sake of making a name and a living for themselves. Lifestyles, language and actions that are detrimental to our children and youth. Have we tasted success so much—those of "us" who have made it—that we have abandoned the strength and knowledge that we gained from struggle?

In the times of slavery and Jim Crow, we black people fell to our knees for help that was above and beyond our capabilities. We needed supernatural help. So we united in prayer and each other. We solidified our moral center and set a standard for trust and a common goal. While our common goal may be the same, somewhere in the progress of success we've drifted away from that standard, moved away from our moral center, and developed our own "evolutionary" standard. In order to get back to a moral center, we will have to put ourselves in strategic positions. Positions of influence with regard to our culture, such as television, radio, music, sports, and entertainment and things that immediately affect and influence people—our people. We are in a constant search for our place in this world and, more importantly, our youth are by what they see, hear, and are told is "normal," due to an evolving world and, even more important, *who* we are listening to and emulating.

Our legacy is not in statues, rap music, sports, or clothes but in our ability to survive and thrive through unity and spirituality. Success is not always evident by being successful if it goes against our moral principles. We must do a better job at explaining what success and wealth and affluence (not influence) really means. To have more constructive and, more importantly, morally centered and spiritually minded role models for our youth is critical, though it will be done against a strong current of do-it-yourselfers and think-for-yourselfers, a culture of those who feel that freedom is the ability to do what is right in your own eyes.

To those of you who are on point, who guide us in the right direction and are not afraid to call us out, I thank you. What I write, I've learned from you. We must get and stay polished. We must understand before we take a stand because ignorance is a personal choice.

—D. Steve Walker

Introduction

While walking the streets of Rome, Italy, one warm July day in 2019, I came upon a faceless, raceless, ethnicity-less person positioned in an unavoidable place, where no one could miss her or him—no assumptions made, as shown on the cover of this book. It seemed obvious to me that the message being conveyed was *not* who this person was but a statement of need. It was like a test for humanity. Am I more important to you than a park bench, or a cute little puppy being walked by a total stranger, or the store windows with expensive clothes, jewelry, and purses, or do you avoid me like the poop dropped by the puppy but immediately and lawfully scooped up by its master? The message? What was the message? It wasn't about how much money could be gathered in his or her tin can. To me, it was simply a cry for help, not necessarily for the person lying there but to draw attention to the blindness of society and its consumption of itself. It showed me the sacrifices one was willing to make to send that message. I'm not trying to make anyone feel guilty or ashamed of their success or of their freedom to choose who they will help or why, but hurting people don't always "holla."

Growing up was more interesting to me than fun. That may sound strange, but feeling alone simply gives you more time to think. It also makes you more vulnerable. You're not yet smart enough to realize it, but your future is being shaped by your present. What you see, hear, and think is molding you into the person you will become, and the hands that shape this clay vessel are the older people around you. The world is a big and strange place, and you watch to see how to be human, how to be what you are, and how to be who you are, especially little boys, trying to earn their "man bones," or little girls, trying to face their own self-esteem.

Being a parent is a privilege, but it's a privilege not given to all, for one reason or another. This is not a book that rails against the abuse and neglect of parents or people in general. It's more of a reflection on how the world changes from generation to generation—a world that we all have a hand in shaping. This is not a book that I wanted to write but a book that wrote me—not words that I made up but words that made me. We are all multifaceted puzzles made up of people we know and knew and bumped into, from the beginning of our existence to now, but ultimately, we are shaped by the choices we make in life.

Life was meant to be fair but never comes out that way, yet you have the ability to be fair. Life is all about choices. I've always believed that God is the ultimate ruler and Creator of life, with the sovereign ability to control all life. He has given us sole charge, however, over one thing and will not interfere with that, although He has the ability to alter it after it's been made, and that is allowing our sovereign will to choose.

As a responsible parent, you are constantly concerned about the growth and choices your child or children make. The first example of who they are comes from their parents. There is so much you want to tell them or warn them against before their own generation shapes and molds them outside of their will. There is simply too much in this world that keeps our youth from focusing on what is important to them, such as their parents and their own personal responsibilities. There are too many challenges to parents' responsibilities and authority. The minds of our youth are on parties, going places, having fun, and living their lives, and there is too much competition against rules and common sense.

Many of our children are like a car with no reverse. They seldom look back any farther than their own lives, as opposed to the life that got them to where they are now. Yet too many parents support that because of anger over where they came from, their life experiences as parents, and the need to not let their children go through what they went through, therefore enabling that type of thinking from our youth. Some parents justify their actions by comparing themselves and their children to the impossible odds presented by those of another race or culture. Even as they grow into adults, there seems to always be something that parents need to tell their children about life and its traps and snares and parents' constant efforts to point them in the right direction.

But there always seems to be little time and always one more thing you'd like to say to your children before you die, knowing that you will not be with them always. There are times when they call you, brimming with good news or filled with sadness over a sick friend or the untimely death of a friend. They may come to you or call you to ask for help in making a decision that, to you, is small but to them is the biggest decision of their lives. They know that you are the only one with certain memories that no one else knows, and no one understands but you two. Tears from your children's eyes rolled down their cheeks but didn't hit the ground because you were always there to catch them. They are always in your heart; there is much to say before you go.

He who feeds the roots feeds the tree, but even with feeding a tree, there is a limit to how high a tree will grow. There is a reason why a tree will never reach the sky. We must learn to accept our limitations while we continue to feed the tree. The book of Matthew 3:10 says, "The axe is already at the root of the trees, and every tree that does not produce good fruit will be cut down...." Feed the root, and you feed the tree. Destroy the root, and you destroy the tree.

Our trees are our young and new generations, and they are being misguided, poisoned by a technology that heals and destroys at the same time, while being infected with the new god of science that pushes our roots from the influences of spirituality, humanity, and family to an independent society of do-it-yourselfers. From our political and democratic processes, to how we approach humanity and lack of respect, to an ever-present corruption of our historical belief systems, in this world we gain more knowledge than wisdom.

As black people, we were a spiritual people who prayed our way out of bondage. Now, we bear witness to generations of youth who not only left their first love—God—but who never knew Him. As Americans, while we hold our heads down, examining our roots from both sides of the cameras, let us not forget to look up at what is happening to our trees. The root of the tree is what gives the tree stability and sustenance. What are we feeding our trees? A better question is, *who* is feeding our trees? He who feeds the roots feeds the trees.

The statements, words, and views, personal or by others, in these chapters are my own walk-through-life ventures and thoughts, as I too ponder the essence of life's challenges and opportunities. Don't be offended or overly impressed.

Chapter 1

If I'm Wrong, Tell Me

My wonderful mom, Sylvia Marie (Melinda) Sweezer-Walker, left this world July 4, 2018, for a heaven that probably had a sign at the entrance that read, "Leave all of your troubles at the gate before entering." When I was just a little boy, she would always sit and talk to me about her problems, mostly about the world and its effect on her children. She would have deep conversations with me, and though I didn't understand the depth of what she was saying, I knew from the worried expressions on her face that it wasn't good and that she was always worried about something bigger than I could help her with—unless she had some candy she was trying to get rid of.

But the one thing that she would always say to me after each talk was a statement that left me hanging every time. She would always look me in the eyes before she said it: "If I'm wrong, tell me." I could never respond to that comment, but I knew it was a cry for help, and I couldn't help her. I also knew that it was a statement of trust. She was asking me to correct her or to help her make a choice between right and wrong, a choice of which way she should go or what she should do. She wanted a right choice that she could live with.

As an adult, I now look back on it and realize that she was probably just venting—thinking out loud but still a cry for help. To this day, that statement haunts me. I often find myself asking the same question. Perhaps it's the same cry for help to a world that can't understand what I'm saying to it, a world only looking for that which satisfies itself. At some point, I guess we are all guilty of that from time to time, but it wears you out.

Mom's absence, conversations, and that question made me ponder another question. Can anyone benefit from my life as I did from hers? Has anyone benefited from your life? The value of a life is not only in how you live it but in how much of it you give away, how much was stolen or taken from you, or how much you take with you when you die, thinking that your life had no real value to anyone. Do you believe that God never had a plan for your life, or that the plan He has included only you? That plan doesn't end until you die, and as long as you are alive, that plan is still in effect.

Like Little Red Riding Hood (emphasis on "The Hood"), you always seem to find yourself running through the woods of life, having to go through something bad to get to something good. And if you can't see the forest for the trees to find your way, it's usually because you're too close to the tree in front of you. Sometimes you have to take a step back in order to keep going forward, in order to see the fullness of what you're facing.

The book of Psalms 10 3:16 says that we humans are like a flower. The wind blows over it, and it's gone, and its place remembers it no more.

Life is like a chair. It has no favorites because if you get up, it'll accept any butt that sits on it.

In the Bible, there was a reason that Job suffered; or that Joseph was thrown into that pit; or that the children of Israel were enslaved; or that Ruth had to glean from a field; or that Christ suffered on a cross. Take none of it for granted. Life doesn't just happen. *We* didn't just happen. And understand this: for every beginning, there is an end. On one end, there's life. On the other end is death. Don't be caught "off God." Always stay "on God"—a play on words, but you know what I mean.

But if I'm wrong, tell me.

Chapter 2

Relationships

What is the hardest job of all required of humankind? It's been said that being a parent is the most difficult job in the world. As a parent myself, I'd agree that it is difficult, but I believe that establishing and maintaining healthy and loving relationships is the most difficult job in the world—not just with your children but with the races, countries, families, and people in general. Why can't we all just get along? The world has lost many more "relationships" than they have children. Our children are expected to be properly raised and taught, then to move out and on with their lives. Relationships were meant to last forever—friends, family, and especially marriage relationships.

Henry David Thoreau once said, "There is no more fatal blunder than he who consumes the greater part of his life getting his living," having to spend the better, stronger and most active part of his life working for a living. Journalist Bill Moyers once remarked that man is not looking for the meaning of life but for the experiences of life—happiness, love, joy, a sliver of peace. Those things that support one's will to live and to live a good and meaningful life. Reverend Billy Graham once said, "Peace is that glorious and wondrous time when all the world stands around, reloading." You soon realize that the most important things in life are not *things* at all but people and relationships. Therefore, the most important part of a relationship is not who left us but what was left behind.

Television journalist Charlie Rose once said that the way you solidify immortality is through legacy. Those are the memories, the good times, laughter, love, and support we receive from good people. He also realized that one mistake can erase your entire past and your good works and add an irrevocable stain to your legacy. That would be OK, except that what's good or bad is left up to the majority opinion of those with similar yet unrevealed circumstances that are otherwise rewarded. How soon we are forgotten, how slowly we are forgiving, and how fast we are judged.

Relationships have become like a gumball machine. You see (visualize) what you want—all of its various shapes, sizes, and colors. You invest hard-earned money into it, turn (or work) it, and you expect to receive and enjoy your prize.

Many of us no longer marry because we love each another—*love* was once defined by Pastor Tony Evans as "passionately and righteously seeking the well-being of another"—but we marry for selfish reasons and sometimes only for the things we want out of the marriage. Marriage is an accepted, binding, bilateral commitment or covenant, in which partners attain the legal and moral rights to express and act on their wants and needs from each other—companionship, financial stability, intimacy; these offer tangible love. And since true love—an emotional love with tangible benefits—was not the primary reason for both, when those things of tangible love diminish (e.g., companionship becomes questionable—trust; money gets funny; sex is bartered), so goes the relationship and then goes the marriage.

Marriage is only the beginning of a relationship process. It is 100 percent work, 100 percent of the time, twenty-four/seven, 365 days a year. We put everything we've got into what we love or have to do. We love our spouses, but we work hard for everything else. Working hard used to be a good thing, a positive thing, a blessing. It kept us in shape physically and emotionally. It gave us longevity.

There are no breaks in a marriage! When done right, it's a beautiful thing to be a part of.

Love. In my years of living, learning, and gaining wisdom, the two toughest commitments in the world, in my opinion, are being a Christian and falling in love. They both require an enormous amount of courage, faith, strength, understanding, and self-control. God rewards faith, but love is always a work in progress. The only pure love now is the love of God for His people.

Is it humanly possible to love someone unconditionally? To love without conditions, requirements, limits, rules, responsibilities, or consequences? That kind of love can only be done by one who has control and the ability to change your present condition at will. We are incapable, due to sin, of this kind of pure love. Love is no longer pure but diluted with tolerance. We don't truly love anymore. We tolerate each other. There would otherwise be no need to draw a line down the middle of a sheet of paper if love was pure. So we compromise. We agree to disagree. Somehow, we manage to make it work. The Bible says that a man should love his wife as Christ loved the church and, yes, be willing to die for her.

When Peter told Christ how much he loved Him and was willing to die for Him, all of that changed when Peter was identified during Christ's capture, and Peter walked away. If a man is willing to stand in front of a train for his wife, it is not because of love. It is because of an obligation and dedication to the Word of God that says it. However, while the book of Matthew says that a woman should respect her husband, it is as hard to tell a woman (wife in a marriage) to sit down (respect) and be a wife (lady), as it is hard to tell a man (husband in a marriage) to stand up (love) and be a husband (man), because neither wants to do it until the other does it first (trust).

Learn to agree to disagree with respect. That's diluted trust. I understand the concept of a strong woman—her attempt to maintain her dignity and self-esteem—but it's like having a Porsche that's capable of going 250 miles per hour where the speed limit is

70 miles per hour. Just because you can go that fast doesn't mean you have to. You won't need to use most of that speed.

To put a man down emotionally with punches and bruises to his manhood and ego, even without physical scars or evidence of abuse, is just as damaging and ungodly as a man physically hitting a woman. The same principal applies to the strength (instead of speed) of a man. Though you have it, Mr. King of Your Castle, if you handle your business right, you'll not need most of it.

Also, you can't expect something from one another if you don't ask for it, such as communication. Let a man be a man. Some of us learn from our mistakes, as well as from the voice and actions of a good woman. In the words of Dr. Lois Evans (God rest her soul) to her husband, Dr. Tony Evans, "We are not here to compete with one another but to complete one another." So true. Bravo! The only caveat I have for that statement is that each individual, before coming together, should work on completing themselves first, not dragging their faults and history into a relationship.

A major issue with marriage is that we spend more time on preparation and wedding plans than on how to maintain the marriage—how to get him or her instead of how to keep him or her. It's the same mistake we make with money or anything of value to us. It's much like a car—we may be able to afford to buy it, but we shouldn't get it until we know that we can afford to maintain it. In order to do that, we need to know what its needs are and if we can honestly maintain those needs.

If you can't maintain a high-maintenance person, you shouldn't marry a high-maintenance person. Otherwise, you will either start to take advantage of one another or take each other for granted. Plan first. Communicate. Ask questions like, "What is important to you in a marriage?" Be honest in your answers. If sex is important to you, your wife should be sexy. If eating right is important to you, she should be a targeted cook to your specific needs. If cleanliness is important to you, she should be domestic and clean. Similar attributes apply to the man. If financial stability is her thing, her husband should have a job with a plan. If companionship is her thing, her husband should treat her like his best friend—or better. You run to your best friend, not from him or her.

Time isn't a factor because you'll always love and want the best for one another. Your goal should be to make each other better individually for the sake of both you and the marriage. If safety is her thing, her husband should be her knight in shining armor.

Man and woman should come together because they are great and true friends; marriage should just be a bonus. This may sound like it's hard—100 percent work, 100 percent of the time—but marriage is like a large lake. As you stand on its shore (the relationship), you look out and take in its beauty, peacefulness, serenity, and calmness, but once you step into it, there's a drop off. You fall into the lake (marriage), and it takes constant effort to stay afloat. Lot of paddling goes on below while showing constraint above the water. When should you stop paddling? You shouldn't, not as long as you want the marriage. Coast with joy and happiness. Ask yourself if you can do this before you take the plunge and fall in love with someone.

When you reach a point in your life where you want to settle down and get married, the first thing to do is not to look for a man or woman but to start working on you—mentally, physically, and spiritually—so that you may offer to your potential mate the best *you* that you can be, in hopes that the one you meet will prepare the same way. This will make you very aware of your value.

Falling in love? Falling requires letting yourself go so that another force takes over. *In love* is being in the caring arms of one you trust to catch you. Falling takes less effort and no help, unless pushed or pulled as gravity takes over to bring you down. But to reverse that, to get up from a fall, takes and often includes physical strength. You often need help getting back onto your feet because gravity's job is to keep you down. You fall in love with the person you come to expect to catch you, hold you up, or pick you up when you fall, not one who will put you down, let you down, or knock you down on purpose. It will be someone you feel you can trust, someone who will grow and care for you've kids because the marriage process often involves procreation. Proverbs 1:8 implies, "Fathers instruct and mothers teach."

It will be someone to whom you can give joy and from whom you can receive joy in good times and bad. It is usually sad and emotional when you've poured your happiness into someone who took it when he or she left or kept it when you left. You marry for joy; happiness is your responsibility.

When you love someone, your goal is to make that person's life better. If you want to know if a relationship is working or worth the next step, ask yourself if your life is better since you met. Do you feel secure? To know that, you have to communicate honestly. Our fear of communication is not a fear of saying what's on our minds but a fear of how the other person will react to it. The recipient must be willing and ready to receive it. We could get along less aggressively in relationships if we started our sentences with, "I could love you more if ..." you took better personal care of yourself, were more responsible with our finances, went to church with me or the family.

Marriage is two people planting each other like seeds and nurturing and watering each other to grow, but if there is no growth, the seed slowly dies, and nothing comes up. There must be growth; otherwise, what a waste of good ground!

The two most important things a man wants, in a marriage or otherwise, are not sex and more sex. They are respect and honor. Sex is an urge, not a feeling—a consecration, not proof. If a woman respects a man, he'll do anything for her; if she honors a man, there's nothing he won't do for her. Most say that respect must be earned, but that's not totally true. When a woman says "I do" to a man, she automatically and simultaneously gives him respect as a husband, leader, and potential father. He has to earn it, however, by living up to that respect, but he enters that marriage, biblically, with respect. He is to be honored and respected, based on that covenant of marriage and the responsibility as the head. And when he asks a woman to marry him, he is vowing to love and protect her as well.

There is always an action before a reaction. Before you say "I do," you must first say "I will." The pervasive thinking on this goes this way: "I am your husband, and you then must be submissive and trusting of me. You are my wife, and I must treasure, protect you, value you, and value your opinion and accept your help." That may be why the woman is the one to say "I do," and the man is the one who asked the woman to marry him. She says, "Yes, I will," because the man already comes with a signed obligation to love his wife as Christ loved the church and to be willing to die for her.

The question on the floor now is, will you say "Yes, I will" before you say "I do"? *I will* says I will trust, obey, and submit. This agreement is totally your choice. In a relationship, there will be some things that you just don't cover—things that you communicate with one another before the other is done and things that you don't—but the relationship and you have to be in the mindset to recover.

Men are at a higher level of expectation than women are. We men are expected to be the protector, to buy flowers, to pay the tab (even during the marriage, though finances are combined), to open doors, to have a job as opposed to chasing our dreams. With women there is an assumption of gratitude of things that she is "supposed" to do, like domestic chores, taking care of the kids, and cooking the meals. In the current generation, mindsets have changed to an agreement on things or the understanding that there is no head of the house, with all being equal, but the precontracted responsibilities of Adam doesn't change and cannot be abdicated. A little respect goes a long way.

As an addendum, may I say that since we are in a culture of what is considered by many as an assault on black men, the question of what a black man wants surfaces often in the hearts of many black women who desire a relationship with a strong and loving black man. The answer to this question is basically the same but seems different because it has been considered missing from relationships with black men. As stated above, respect and honor top the list. Many black men feel less respected and less honored by black women, especially in a culture of strong black women who feel less of a need for such a man, openly; subconsciously, they want the leadership of a strong black man but feel the need to show strength over weakness to avoid being used.

Many women would love for a man to take over and be in the front of their relationship and their lives, but history and trust is the gatekeeper. A black man wants deep love, commitment, and surrender. A black man wants a loving family. A black man wants a sanctuary, a place to respectfully reign, a castle, a home with peace and tranquility, with all of its imperfections and problems to solve. A black man wants to be depended on and held responsible. He wants to be lifted up when he comes through and lovingly supported when he fails. A black man wants someone to love and give all to; he wants a reason to work hard, which is what sustains him. A black man wants a black queen who deserves the title, with respect and honor till death. His only difference is being black and male.

I am not trying to create a fight between who's more important than the other, but I did run across an interesting article on the *Inside Man* July 25, 2014 titled, "So Why Are Men Disposable?" It said,

> *Biologically speaking, men are much more disposable than women ... because one man can father thousands of children, we don't need many men. ... men are generally stronger than women ... and have an innate protective role ... though domestic violence is not innate.*

It does raise questions about the evolution of our society and man's fight (though not literally) to regain his place. Marriage comes with it hierarchy (i.e., God, Jesus, Holy Spirit—three in one, angels, man, woman, animals, nature), and when that hierarchy is disturbed, it will always create chaos.

Gender equality? Man was created in the image of God (male). Woman was created in the image of humanity (human), as the first birth was a woman from a man, performed by Dr. God. Both are equal in humanity and Christ but not in authority and hierarchy, except outside of God's will, which includes living one's life outside of one's lane as a man or woman.

Submissiveness has become a dirty word. Submissiveness means to be willing to trust and submit to your husband's authority as head, per biblical standards. It is to know, understand, and stay in our lanes to otherwise avoid an accident. It is to complete one another, as previously discussed, not to compete with one another—but only after you feel complete within yourself. Two broken pieces need to be solid and strong enough to create and come together as two whole pieces; otherwise, they can be penetrated at its weakest point. It is to assist one another, not insist on each other.

Lastly—but most importantly—please understand this: when a woman is looking for a man with whom to spend the rest of her life, she expects him to be loving, understanding, trustworthy, and strong. She expects him to be a good man—not perfect but at least a good man. But here's the problem: women aren't the only ones looking for a good man. Everyone's looking for a good man. Many of our boys, young men, and older adult men have never had a good man in their lives. Deep down, many men are looking for a good man. Many boys don't have a historical view of what a good man should be or how he should behave.

Many grew up with no man or father in the house or in an unhealthy family unit. Unless they had a respected coach or a mentor, they have nothing to fall back on. Men struggle to be men—the definition being what the world shows on television, in media, and in man-to-man conversations. They struggle to be the man they are expected to be, not showing weakness or vulnerability, especially to the women they so desperately want to please. That's not an excuse for bad behavior, but it's a sad and realistic point to keep in the back of your mind.

And speaking of bad behavior, as weird as this may sound, allow a good controlled argument. Feelings may get hurt, but sometimes, feelings need to be hurt in order to get out the truth or pent-up pressure inside that can burst a pipe. Know, however, that you love one another first. An argument is just communication without borders. The biggest regret will be never having expressed your feelings. Take time to listen to each other during your argument. Process what your partner says before you respond and then respond truthfully, but choose your words carefully. Don't be too proud to say "I'm sorry," even if you meant what you said.

Always remember that it's not what you say but how you say it. Learn to forgive, even if you can't forget. If you learn nothing about yourself and the other person from your argument, you've wasted your time. If people don't understand what you're going through when you blow up, they may see it as an attack on them personally.

True love is rarely tested in the good times but is always validated in the bad times. If you can get over yourself, you can get over each other and others too. Commit to being better.

Let me flip the proverbial coin for a second to say that, for many, marriage is not a necessity or a driving force. Many people lose valuable time while living life, looking for someone that they feel will make their lives better or normal (whatever that is!). Seeing your friends, coworkers, classmates, or church members date, get married, and have children at an early age can be threatening to your path in life, but it shouldn't be. Never getting married or being a "late bloomer" is not a curse, nor does it make you unwanted or incapable of finding a mate. Many rush into that dream created by others, only to find themselves miserable and maybe even pausing or bypassing their dreams or true purposes in life.

It is OK to reject the typical lifestyle on life's so-called timeline. You must feel comfortable with your decision and not be pressured into a lifestyle that's doesn't fit at this point in your life, if ever. You are not strange because you are a woman and not married and don't have children; you are not strange if you don't even want to be married or have children. Being happy is a choice that is validated by decisions you make in your life, not by persuasive assumptions and fables. Now you can breathe! (UBU) You Be You.

Chapter 3

A Time to Live, a Time to Die

Is there really a time appointed for humans to die, or does only God know when we will die, knowing our end at our beginning, while understanding human free will and sinful ways and His having the ability to affect or change it at will? While we humans have attempted to interpret God's Word, we cannot interpret or predict God's specific will or decisions at any given time. We must simply trust Him. Remember that He did grant Hezekiah fifteen more years of life at his appointed time of death. It's just a thought.

We must keep in mind that when we exercise our bodies or minds, when we take our vitamins or prescription medicines, when we get over a cold or make it through an operation, when chemotherapy works or the pacemaker kicks in just at the right time, or when a baby is born or Grandma or Grandpa use a cane or get a new knee or hip, we are only postponing the inevitable. We will die, as it is appointed unto man. Be surprised but do not be shocked. Love hard, love deeply, but always be ready to let go.

In living life, the significance is the destination, where God wants you to be. The moral of the story is to enjoy the journey. The journey is always the preparation for the destination. Don't worry yourself to death about life. Don't worry about age and how life is slipping away and how we should enjoy life while we can. Live like you are going to die, but live morally and responsibly. Life itself is a privilege, not something that God owes you. The most important person is always the person in front of you. While facing one another, both of you are accountable for one another. The past is gone, and the future's not promised to us; therefore, all we have is now.

Know that you are loved. Let those close to you know that you love them in whatever way is comfortable to you. A wonderful, lovely, and compassionate life-loving friend and coworker of mine went to be with the Lord in 2018. Her name was Sundra, nicknamed "*Sundy*", McWoods. Many friends, associates, church members, and coworkers attended her retirement party. It was a wonderful time of celebration, but it was obvious to most—and no secret—that Sundy was not in the best of health. I went to her at the family table that was set for her in the middle of the floor, as did many, and congratulated her and hugged her, and I witnessed her signature smile. But it was what she said to me that has haunted me to this day. With her big eyes and wide smile, she said, "Don, I didn't know so many people loved me!"

Let's do better. Never hold on to people so tightly that it becomes painful or hold them so loosely that they slip away, especially before you tell them that you love them.

Chapter 4

Dark Places

When you don't talk to or advise someone in an unhealthy situation, using the excuse that you haven't walked in their shoes or don't know what is really going on in the dark places of their lives, is simply a false justification to not act. People need to be encouraged in their current situations, even without your knowing their dark secrets, because the dark will never give up directions to the light. The voice that leads that person to the door has to come from outside the door. You don't have to go into their dark places to get them out because, whether inside or outside, they must want to come out. That reason could very well come from outside of their dark places.

For many, it is the challenge of changing their present situation or changing themselves. It leads to insanity. Viktor Frankl noted in his book *Man's Search for Meaning*, "When we are no longer able to change our situation, it is at that time we must then change ourselves." But what happens when the situation or thing we are trying to change is us? If we refuse to change ourselves, we stay in constant conflict within ourselves. We will eventually drive ourselves insane.

Insanity is not the state of being out of your mind; it is being trapped inside your mind. It is you wanting out. It is said that there is a time when the mind is dealt such a blow that it hides itself in insanity. It will simply retreat from reality. The age-old unanswerable question of *why* is really a subtle acronym (WHY) for the question, "Who Hurt You?" For many, that question should be asked of and by ourselves. Ask yourself who hurt you and then forgive them. Then forgive yourself. Then change your behavior. Then change your life.

If you can't forget, then forgive—for you. You want answers. The answer to a problem is rarely the solution to your problem. The solution is your ability to accept that answer. You see, stress is not a product of issues in your life. Stress is the by-product of unresolved issues. We all crave approval—for someone to believe in us or what we are doing or the message we are giving.

Exodus 18:22 instructs us to bare (lighten) one another's burdens, but don't carry (take) their load. That will make their load lighter because they will share it with you. Exodus 18:23 says that if you do this, as God so commands you, you will be able to stand the strain.

Sometimes, all that we're looking for is this:

A Place to Land

I knew I eventually had to leave this home, this city, but it wasn't because of what I hated, it was because of what I loved. I couldn't stand by and watch what I love be destroyed. It was just too much. I knew that it would eventually destroy me as well. To see bodies wither, education wasted, common sense ignored, mediocrity applauded and poverty welcomed as a close friend. To look down and see my feet not moving, my hands not reaching out, my eyes not focused though prompted to move forward, always forward. I knew I didn't belong here. Here, where I was born but not raised. Educated but not taught, protected but not liberated. Free but not told that I could fly. Like a new born baby at birth I needed to be 'PUSHed' out, not pulled in many directions. I needed a path to follow or I would wither away like the rest of them. So I left. Leaving behind the only life I knew, that I might find a new life and survive. I needed something to live for. To be surrounded by living people. To experience life. I needed a Purpose. I needed a direction. I had extended my wings and I few away. But now, what I need is a place to land.

(DS Walker)

When the pressures of life come upon us, we may transfer our burdens, which we gave to the Lord by faith, back from Him and onto ourselves, even though it is at that time that we should draw nearer to Him. We should be ready and able to accept whatever the Lord gives us, knowing that His love for those of us who fear Him endures forever, and we should be confident that His grace is sufficient. Avoid entering that dark place where God plans His next step for you. It's like the holy of holies, but there's no rope for anyone to pull you out. Though we are fearfully and wonderfully made, our minds are limited in their capacity to handle God's thoughts.

When you blow air into a balloon, you soon realize that it can hold only so much air before it destroys itself. Its capacity is simply limited by design. When I try to think of a God in terms of a person who "knows the exact number of hairs" on every person's head; who can hear and answer the prayers of every person—billions of people—anytime, anywhere; who created, built, and controls not only this rock we live on but every aspect of life—human, animal, inanimate objects, stars, sky, galaxies, angels—and all with the power of death and life, it can stretch one's mind to a capacity to where it destroys itself.

Like a balloon, our minds can only hold, imagine, or think to a limited capacity; after that, the mind reaches a point where it will destroy itself, unless we stop at the point of faith. Going crazy doesn't necessarily mean that you are out of your mind; it's just the opposite—where you literally get trapped *inside* your mind. At that point, just before the balloon pops, a decision must be made. Accept it by faith, reject it by science, or *pop*! We are not little gods. We have limits. We can only take in so much information, so much pressure, so much love, so much hate, so much pain, so much failure, and, yes, so much success before we pop.

Author Joseph Campbell, as quoted in the 1991 Diane K. Osbon published "Reflection on the Art of Living: A Joseph Campbell Companion" once said, *"We must be willing to let go of the life we've planned, so as to accept the life that is waiting for us."* Giving up our independence is one of the hardest things we humans can do. We want something to hold on to, just in case what we are holding on to doesn't hold on to us.

Mark Twain once wrote, "The two most important days in our lives are the day we were born and the day we find out why." Until then, we drift and float, looking for a place to land. Some never find that place; they just land.

God is with you no matter where you are. Your arms are getting tired, your eyesight is getting dimmer, and time waits on no one. Just land. Now, take a deep breath, and live.

From darkness into the light, we go.

Chapter 5

Truth Be Told

The one thing that offends people the most is the truth. A comfortable lie is preferred. Job said, "How painful are honest words" (Job 6:25). The truth hurts sometimes. Truth is the biggest danger for which we should prepare our children because truth hurts the most of all and is the most painful and challenging thing they will ever face. Remember the famous line from the 1992 movie *A Few Good Men*: "You can't handle the truth!"? The truth holds us accountable. Author and speaker Dr. Tony Evans once defined truth as "a fixed absolute standard by which reality is to be measured—but has now been distorted by sin."

Our children are living and growing up in a "learned" world, where wisdom is not accepted as a legitimate form of learning. It takes the ability to be quiet and to listen and the examination of opinion. Children's constant struggle is a search for their identity that is different from their parents' generation. They do ignorant things to set themselves apart and, therefore, claim ignorance as their difference and their identity as their normal. Many will embrace homosexuality as their own to separate themselves from an underclass to go to a protected special class that allows them justification for their feelings of being different. They go from different to special, and anyone who disagrees with them or their lifestyles will soon feel the wrath of an open-door society.

Our youth now live—we all live—in a world of comments turned into reality because untruth is repeated so much that it becomes real to them and us. Some people may say, "Don't spoil children. They need to suffer a little bit." Really? While I am all for not sparing the rod—or as Proverbs 19:18 says, "Discipline your children for in that there is hope; do not be a party to their death"— life has its own built-in struggles. Trust me—they won't miss a thing.

People are more willing to risk the consequences of a lie than they are comfortable with the truth. We have come to value the friendship more than the friend. Someone might say, "I love what we have—the friendship—more than I love you, the friend." The truth saves lives. A lie covers the truth. Sometimes the biggest lie we can tell is silence. We have not conditioned ourselves to accept truth and failure as part of life. We are offended by both.

Society is confused by seeing bad people do good things. Society is also confused by seeing good people do bad things. We are blinded by the glamor of sin. What's normal to us now was not meant to be normal in God's perfect world. We have now adopted, adapted to, and accepted as normal the norms of an imperfect and sinful world. We are living in a fool's paradise.

The Bible does not say that God will win in the end. Truth be told, it tells us—reminds us—that God has already won, and we need to catch up. Not only is God in control, but there was never a battle on His part. Yes, we will lose a few battles in life, but we live like we are going to win, when we should be living like we have already won!

Chapter 6

From Guilt to Grace

My declaration of sin: "I declare that I have traded in my halo for grace."

Guilt is a blindfold that keeps you from seeing the hand of God's grace in your life. To many, it's like a makeup test they missed or failed. A. W. Tozer remarked in his book *The Root of the Righteous*:

> We boast in the Lord but watch carefully that we never get caught depending on Him … Pseudo faith always arranges a way out to serve in case God fails. … It would be a tragedy indeed to come to the place where we have no other but God and find that we had not really been trusting God during the days of our earthly sojourn.

The opposite of that is that, by grace, we give credit to God for everything that we have and do up front, and we acknowledge our dependence on Him. Guilt has a way of eating us alive from the inside out, like a worm, as it did to Herod in Acts 12:23.

First John 1:9 says that "if we confess our sins, He is faithful and righteous to forgive us our sins and to cleanse us from all unrighteousness."

But interestingly, Psalm 32:5 says,

> I acknowledged my sin to You, And my iniquity I did not hide; I said, "I will confess my transgressions to the Lord"; And You forgave the 'guilt' of my sin.

If God is true—and I believe He is—we who believe and confess are forgiven. Due to our human frailties, sinful nature, and promises we can't keep, however, we harbor the guilt of not being able to achieve the perfection of our confessions, which bears the reflection of unbelief and mimics the words of Satan in the garden of Eden in (NIV) Genesis 3:4: "You will not certainly die."

The purpose of redemption and the cross is restoration. Restoration is only done to things that are broken, worn, and sometimes unrecognizable outside of the original and true form.

It is not the dos and don'ts of the Law that gets God's attention or His provision of mercy—we are not capable, in our sinful state, of maintaining that or of pleasing God in that way—but the recognition and appreciation of grace. That is what garners and sustains our freedom. Don't be pushed into a corner by the guilt of what you are not capable of doing. Know that you were made free of guilt by grace. Grace frees us to choose. It silences needless guilt and removes self-imposed shame. Few people realize better than non-Christians how guilt-ridden many Christians are. We temper our guilt by doing random acts of kindness. Doing good things cannot be done to gain grace but are of grace as works follows grace, not the reverse.

Grace is a symptom of gratefulness.

> … "If you hold to my teaching, you are really my disciples. 32. Then you will know the truth and the truth will set you free" (John 8:31–32) NIV

You are not captive; you just think you are, and the truth shall not set you free (that's physical). The word *set* says that you are in a cage and want to get out to freedom. The word *make* says that there is no cage; it's all in your mind. Jesus has already set you free. You must make yourself free by believing that you are free.

Harriet Tubman was reported to have been asked how many slaves she believed she set free via the Underground Railroad. She said she wasn't sure but knew that she could have set many more free, if they had "believed" that they were slaves. Do we, as Christians, suffer the same fate? Do we not *believe* that we are free? Their slavery was all they knew; it was the norm for them. To violate that slavery was to take away what they saw as freedom. They were bound by mental slavery.

The Law binds you; grace sets you free. Controversially speaking, could we be causing the church and the Bible itself to be our idols, worshiping them instead of what they represent—our God? Ironically, the dictionary defines the Bible as "an image of a deity other than God."

As I stated earlier, the dos and don'ts of the Law do not get God's attention or His provision of mercy but the recognition and appreciation of grace! That is what garners and justifies our freedom. Many Christians are guilt-ridden by their actions in public, as opposed to their actions in their private moments and spiritual places.

Do not become a slave to freedom—the ability to do anything. We live with both the blessings and the risks of grace. Disbelief is holding you captive. The cage is either disbelief or guilt. Guilt follows belief. Freedom is the release that allows others to be who they are meant to be—different from me! Never forget that grace came with a high price—Christ's death on the cross. Psalm 85:2 (NLT) says, "You forgave the guilt of your people—yes, you covered all their sins."

Knowledge breaks the chains of guilt. Acceptance releases you from its bondage. Understanding heals the wounds.

We are one part of a body—the body of Christ. We suffer not because we are different but because we are unique, each given a gift that the other cannot understand because it is unique to each one, given to us through the Holy Spirit. It's very difficult for us to give it up because it has been made such a part of us. We must recognize it and control it, realizing that while our gift is unique to us, it is unacceptable to and misunderstood by others. We must respect that without discarding our gift. The only one who can control or help with that is the one who gave it, the Holy Spirit, triune God.

While people are giving their lives, they're not living their lives. While they are being saved, they're not being delivered. Much of that is guilt, mostly due to a lack of knowledge, the failure to pursue a personal relationship with Christ, and a veiled understanding of His love for us. We are like Christian serial killers. We have so much baggage—so many dead bodies and broken promises—that even if we stopped today, we're still guilty of past crimes that we cannot pay for. We deserve death. Our only hope is a perfect Savior.

Chapter 7

Why Are My Prayers Not Being Answered?

You don't just meander into God's presence with a list of gimmes. There is an honor and a respect that is due His name. There is a thought process that needs to be pondered and a reverence given.

A prayer is gathered thoughts of appreciation, praise, and concerns for yourself and others throughout your day, presented to God at any time of the day or night.

How to Pray

Gather your thoughts of appreciation and thanks throughout your day for whatever life has given you.

Remember God throughout the day for the small things, not to mention the things you don't even know about that He has commanded His angels to do for you and to deliver you from.

Develop a greater awareness of your senses as you walk through life—the abilities and freedoms not afforded others.

Notice the outdoors more than the indoors—what God has done more than what humans have done—and give Him the glory He deserves.

Psalms 36 says that God's love reaches to the heavens and His faithfulness to the skies. This statement shouts out to me, "I love you enough to not give you all that you ask of me, as you chose to put your life in My hands, knowing that I know what's best for you and that I will supply all your needs, 'According to His riches in glory by Christ Jesus'" (Philippians 4:19).

> For as the heavens are higher than the earth, So are
> My ways higher than your ways, And My thoughts
> than your thoughts. (Isaiah 55:8–9)

You trust me. You cannot be trusted. I will not give you your request if what you ask for is not best for you.

In a more practical and simplistic understanding, God's Word says in Psalm 36:5 "Your love, LORD, reaches to the heavens, your faithfulness to the skies.". which seems to say that since the heavens are higher than the skies, His LOVE for us is higher and takes precedence over His faithfulness to our requests. In other words, His LOVE for us supersedes any request or prayer that we make to Him that He knows is not good for us.

> But the Lord was with Joseph in the prison and
> showed him His faithful love. (Genesis 39:21)

Evangelical Christian pastor and author Charles "Chuck" Swindoll once noted in one of his devotional statements:

> Our human ways are based on what seems fair.
> We firmly believe that when someone does what is
> right, rewards and blessings result. When someone
> does what is wrong, there are serious consequences,
> even punishment. But that's our way, not necessarily
> God's way. At least not immediately. He's been
> known to allow unfair treatment to occur in the

27

lives of absolutely innocent folks—for reasons far more profound and deeper than they or we could have imagined.

To God, we are a treasure in an abandoned field. Matthew 13:44 speaks of an abandoned field with an abandoned treasure on it. Most look at it as a worthless field, but one man found treasure in that abandoned field. Instead of taking the treasure out, he hid the treasure again and went out and gathered enough money (all that he had) to purchase (more than he deserved) the abandoned property. Those who looked at the property without seeing, knowing, or expecting that treasure was there only saw abandonment, while those who looked deeper—or he who searched with expectation—found the treasure on that property and did not remove it but purchased the whole property that contained the treasure, validating that the property was always worth more. Most people (those who didn't see or hear and would have taken the treasure for themselves) never discovered its true value. This allowed the man to build on and around the property to make it worth much more.

We are the abandoned field in which God saw treasure. He did not simply remove the treasure. He sent Christ to buy the field, seeing that it was smarter to preserve the entire property with the treasure on it than simply to take the treasure off the property, which would still leave an abandoned property.

> But you, when you pray, go into your inner room, close your door and pray to your Father who is in secret, and your Father who sees what is done in secret will reward you. (Matthew 6:6)

Since God already knows all, this time is for you to bear your soul to Him—but for you. Whether naked or clothed, loud or soft, emotional or strong, this time is for you to hear you cry out to God, just as Jesus raised Lazarus not for His benefit but "for the benefit of [you] those standing around."

Ask and ye shall receive, so you've gotta verbally ask, which is simultaneously confessing your need for Him, thus validation Him, your Daddy, as your source. This is what makes Him want to respond to you. Like all daddies, He wants to talk and hang out with you, not just answer your wish list prayers. He, like any good father, wants a personal relationship with you, faults and all. He wants to spend time with you—alone.

God is a God of many directions, and all roads lead to mercy and grace and truth. Is there really such a thing as God not answering our prayers? Yes, no, or wait often seems like a punishment. But I'd rather be punished by God than praised by the devil any day!

In addition to how much God loves you is the question of how much you love or value yourself. The value of anything is based on the price one is willing to pay for it. Value will always supersede cost. If Christ gave His life for those of us who call Him Lord, then how valuable are we to Him, even as compared to the cost He knew He had to pay. He literally pulled us out of the teeth of eternal death, saving us not from Satan's hell (Hell doesn't belong to Satan, nor can Satan send you to hell) but from God's wrath. Heaven and hell belong to God Almighty. A. W. Tozer, in his book *The Root of the Righteous*, said:

> If the devil does come to you and whispers that you are no good, don't argue with him. In fact, you might as well admit it, but then remind the devil: "regardless of what you say about me, I must tell you how the Lord feels about me. He tells me that I am so valuable to Him that He gave Himself for me on the cross!"

If someone tells you that you are nothing, no good, not worth anything, etc., ask that person this question: "Even though you know I am all of these things that you just said, would you still die for me? Jesus thought that I was so worth it that He did. Yet I still suffer from the guilt of sin for which He has forgiven me."

Christ's death on the cross did not relieve us from our sinful ways or sinful nature but from the consequences of our sins. That's mercy. That's grace. You are worth it to Him.

Patience is indeed a virtue. Why did God wait so long before rescuing the children of Israel, His children? Why forty years in the desert? Why two years before letting Joseph out of prison? Why forty years before releasing Moses from the servanthood of Jesse to go to his destiny of releasing the children of Israel from their slavery? Always more whys than answers, yet everything always seems to fall in place. There was a reason that Job suffered, even though the reason was not apparent; or that Joseph was thrown into that well; the children of Israel were enslaved; Ruth had to glean from a field; or that Christ suffered and died on a cross.

God only speaks to *you* when He needs something done. Others will not have heard His words spoken to you and will think that something is wrong with you (such as with Adam, Noah, Moses, Job), questioning your actions, even your sanity, and making you feel all alone and doubting what you're doing. Others may not understand why you do what you do, but if you know God's Word, you can recognize God's voice and even His work. Sometimes, you simply need to be still and know that you are loved.

When you speak to others about the Lord, don't be all Gucci spiritual. Speak so people can afford it!

Chapter 8

Fearfully and Wonderfully Made, with Issues

When we say "fearfully" (apprehensively, timidly, nervously—describes human nature) and "wonderfully" (excellently, extraordinarily, amazingly—and in His image, by the way; God's nature) made, are we referring to the Creator who made us, or that which was created when considering the definitions described? Are we saying that the Creator fearfully and wonderfully made us with the embodiment of fear and of wonder? Obviously, both.

Fear is a great igniter; it's needed to push us forward and give us that drive to survive. God is saying that when that happens, He will always be there to strengthen you and see you through. The book of Jeremiah 1:5 describe how our Creator knew us in and out, from beginning to end, before He made us, just as Romans 5:8 says, "Even while we were yet inners Christ died for us."

He knows our temptations and our fears, our timidity and apprehensions, our strengths and weaknesses and challenges and the time we need to grow (remember, fruit doesn't show up on a planted tree until the roots are firmly established) and trust in the Lord, all built in on purpose. Yet He still made us wonderfully, excellently, and with amazing fearlessness inside (His spirit) that counteracts the fearfulness of our humanity outside.

> For God has not given us a 'spirit' of fear and
> timidity, but of power, love and self-discipline.
> (2 Timothy 1:7 NLT)

That power, love, and self-discipline has to be ignited, and fearfulness is the spark that we need in our human state—to ignite that flame that pushes us to the spirit of power, love, and self-discipline. We "fear" God with that same wonder and excellence.

Psalm 140 continues and validates our fearful needs and dependence on our need for protection, grace, and mercy, yet we maintain the courage to reach out to our wonderful Maker, who wonderfully made us. We are born fearful yet wonderfully still wanting children, knowing that we are birthing our wonderful children into a cruel, dying, and evil world as we know it, prior to the birth of that child, yet we are prepared to protect and fight for our families (as in Nehemiah 4:14).

But fear is real. I ventured up on the roof of my house with a home inspector one morning so that he could show me what he had found. He was very comfortable walking on the rooftop, but I was very cautious. I revealed to him how surprised I was to even be up on the roof because I am deathly afraid of heights.

The inspector asked me, "Why are you afraid of heights?"

"It's because I'm afraid I will fall," I told him.

He retorted, "Then you're not afraid of heights; you are afraid of falling."

I never thought of it that way. Later that day, I pondered that statement. *So I'm not afraid, then, of deep waters or not knowing how to swim. I'm afraid of drowning.* Many are not afraid of the commitment of marriage but are afraid of divorce; they're not afraid to accept Christ but are afraid of the guilt of failing to live up to such high standards. Facing your fears, however, knowing that you are in the will of God, changes everything!

We can be out of a job but know that we are in the will of God and stand strong. We can face a threatening situation but know that we are in the will of God and stand strong. We can have the odds stacked against us but know that we are in the will of God and stand strong. We can even not understand the will of God but know that we are in the will of God. The mind finds it impossible to wrap itself around perfection. Failure is inevitable and is, therefore, fearful to face.

What kind of God do you have if you believe God but don't trust Him? Trusting in the Lord does not come automatically with your being saved. It is a time-consuming struggle that forces you to focus on that which is obligated, willing, and able to save your life. That trust comes only after you have gone through the "boot camp of life." Believing and receiving Christ as your Lord and Savior is your signing up for boot camp. How long you stay in it depends on how long it takes you to trust. Boot camp sends you through trials in order to strengthen you so that you can survive the battles and win the wars.

So count it all as joy when you go through boot camp trials. This does not say be happy for a trial, but when you go through it or when God delivers you through the trial, you face it. You approach it, knowing that you are in the will of God to stand strong. You must know your true fear, and then face it before you can conquer it. Nothing can intimidate those who know that what they believe is based on what God has said. It allows you to stand strong and confident!

Chapter 9

A Time to Rest

Think with me here: to enter into His rest is to enter into or to be a part of His destiny—God's finished plan. I would imagine that when God finished His work of creation, His rest was not in what He had just created but in the joy of what He was going to do with His creation; He visualized their destiny—His final finished work of man living with God forever in perfection. "Enter into my vision of the final destination for man and mankind" which due to Genesis 3 is now a *new* heaven and a *new* earth. The new plan now is to salvage what man has destroyed through disobedience in the garden by way of restoration through the perfection of Jesus Christ. Then the total destruction of sin, back to perfection and giving full authority to our Lord and Savior Jesus Christ. He defeated death, restored back to prominence the promise, and sits at the right hand of the Father, waiting on His finished work to put all control under the feet of Jesus, as is deserved. COVID's ability to shut down and travel around the world in a matter of days, along with Russia's invasion of Ukraine should not be as surprising as it is to those who follow scripture. Matthew 24:6 (NIV) says, "You will hear of wars and rumors of wars, but see to it that you are not alarmed. Such things must happen, but the end is still to come."

We who are saved from God's wrath are dealing with the guilt, as the commandments hang over our heads like an anvil, due to our constant sinning and inability to control our disobedient actions for the one who gave so much—His life—and our not having a full understanding of grace and the new covenant.

So what about us? How does rest play into our human existence? How does our rest benefit God? Is God impressed by the accomplishments made by "trespassing" our time with family or friend or "transgressing" our time with God? The nucleus of rest is *time*, thus a time to rest. No one simply rests. Rest has to be either scheduled voluntarily or caused involuntarily. In this go-get-it world, rest is an expendable commodity, ignored in order to show our diluted determination of endurance and lustful pride of success. Rest is not just sitting still or sleeping. Rest is our time to think and appreciate the good things in life and to realize that no matter where we are in life, things could be worse or better. Rest allows us to be content with the simple things in life while reaching for a better life. We "rest in" our situations, our troubles, our concerns, and our blessings. We rest so that we can power up for the battles ahead. In the book *I Am Not Your Negro* by James Baldwin, we learn that before he moved back to France he quoted, "In America, I was free only in battle, never free to rest, and he who finds no way to rest cannot long survive the battle."

We no longer live to be hundreds of years old, like Moses and Methuselah. Many of us will never reach the day when the cake won't hold all of the candles. Unlike God, we may not rest in order that we may stand back and look at our accomplishment of creating a world, but rest does allow us to slow down; it allows God to give us direction and instruction and to sit with us and whisper our future in our small world, telling us that all is not lost. He ensures you personally that He is there with you.

Indeed, few are those whose hearts are quiet enough to hear God speak. Learn to be patient. Patience is the ability to adjust to the wait, so you might as well rest.

Chapter 10

Are Thoughts and Prayers Enough?

Her child was missing. Tears rolled down her cheeks, and the shattered sound of her broken heart drowned out the silent voices that disturbed her inner peace. Her drained spirit gave her no answers, and she wept. Gathering herself unapologetically for empathetic well-wishers, she looked straight into the news cameras and uttered these words: "I don't need your thoughts and prayers!"

It's the newest version of "I'll pray for you," or "I'm sorry for your loss." Sending "thoughts and prayers"—the latest in clichés uttered by many who have no spiritual thoughts and no idea of how to pray or to whom. That statement mostly is not meant for the person who is hurting but a way to free the speaker from action—a way of soothing the guilty mind. While works can never get you into heaven, faith without works is indeed dead. Works are the evidence of faith and the hope embedded in action.

Thoughts require one to stop and meditate on a specific person or point. They require the use of the mind, heart, and body.

Thoughts are—or should be—made up of things that are true, honorable, just, pure, lovely, and commendable (Philippians 4:8).

Thoughts that are not conformed to this world but are transforming (Romans 12:2).

Thoughts that are set on the Spirit (Romans 8:5–6).

Thoughts that come from wisdom and not those who think themselves wise (1 Corinthians 3:18).

Thoughts that are filtered for understanding through the Lord (2 Timothy 2:7).

Thoughts that come from the heart of the righteous (Proverbs 15:28).

Thoughts that are not anxious about anything but prayerful about everything (Philippians 4:6).

Thoughts that come from a joyful heart, not from a crushed spirit (Proverbs 17:22).

Thoughts that give one liberty with contentment that stays with you (Hebrews 13:5).

Thoughts that make the tree good and its fruit good because it comes from one who is known by its fruit (Matthew 12:33–37).

Thoughts that are of power and love, not of fear (2 Timothy 1:7).

Thoughts that give us the power that allows us to overcome all things through Him who gives us strength (Philippians 4:13).

Thoughts that are free from bitterness, wrath, anger, and slander but are tenderhearted and forgiving (Ephesians 4:31–32).

Thoughts that you believe to be true (Matthew 21:22).

Thoughts that are not of your thoughts or of your ways but are higher than your ways and higher than your thoughts (Isaiah 55:8–9).

Thoughts that you are not fearful of the wind carrying them to the ears of God (Ecclesiastes 10:20).

Thoughts from a sober mind full of grace that brings hope (Peter 1:13).

Thoughts that even renew your mind (Ephesians 4:23).

These are thoughts that are needed.

But what about prayers? Prayer should be something that assures a person that God can take him or her from between a rock and a hard place to a pillow and a soft bed.

First, prayers should be *for* people and not *to* people. You don't pray to inanimate objects or to highly educated minds but to the one who created both. People need to know that you speak on their behalf to one who can go above and beyond all that we can think or do—one who cannot be influenced or overruled but has your best interest in mind; one who loves you enough to give you what you need but not give you what you want for your best interest. Many see God as a huge ball of love who can tolerate any mistake and forgive every sin. As Chuck Swindoll once said, "He who loves us most knows us best. He who knows us best cares the most." No man, object, or beast can do that. That takes God—the only one and true God, Abba Father who art in heaven.

A prayer is gathered thoughts of appreciation and concerns for yourself and others throughout your day, presented to God as an offering of thanks at any time of the day or night.

Preparation for Prayer

Gather your thoughts throughout your day of appreciation for life.

Remember the Lord throughout the day for the small things.

Develop a greater awareness of your senses.

Notice the outdoors more than the indoors and what God has done more than what humans have done, and give God His props.

Prayers don't have to be long, drawn out, loud, or impressive, but they should be honest and truthful. Matthew 6:6 says,

> But you, when you pray, go into your inner room, lose your door and pray to your Father who is in secret, and your Father who sees what is done in secret will reward you.

It would seem to me that since God already knows all, this time of prayer is for you to bear your soul *to* Him but *for* you. Whether naked or clothed, loud or soft, emotional or strong, this time is for you to hear yourself cry out to God. Jesus raised Lazarus not for Jesus's benefit but "for the benefit of [you and] those standing around." You see, whenever you pray for others, you simultaneously pray for yourself. Ask, and ye shall receive, so you must verbally ask, which simultaneously confesses your need for Him, thus validating Him, your Daddy, as your source. This is what makes God want to respond to you. God is the ultimate daddy. Like any good father, He wants a personal relationship with you, faults and all. He wants to spend time with you.

Guilt holds back many from prayer. Guilt is a blindfold that keeps you from seeing the hand of God's grace in your life. It is not the dos and don'ts of God's Law that gets God's attention or His provision of mercy. We are not humanly capable of perfection in our sinful state of mind and existence, but we *are* capable of the recognition and appreciation of God's grace and liberty. Knowledge frees the chains of guilt. Acceptance releases you from its bondage. Understanding heals the wounds.

Love is not what you do for someone but what you give to someone from an act of the will. You give to others what they desire or need, not what they want. So if they say that they do not want your thoughts and prayers, it seems they are saying, deep down, that they don't *want* your thoughts and prayers but they *need* your thoughts and prayers because they need to heal. Einstein once said, "Time exists so that everything wouldn't happen all at once." Healing takes time; it rarely happens all at once. A. W. Tozer once said, "It is doubtful whether God can bless a man greatly until He has hurt him deeply." It is said that the ground will accept only strong roots—roots strong enough to dig down and long enough to allow what is on top to survive; that takes time and work.

We now live in a world where new generations are tired of praying for change, going to church, and hearing sermons on love, peace, and patience because they are told that the things that are happening today have been happening for centuries—things that their grandparents and ancestors went through. They look at today and see that we are still going through the same things—poverty, racism, cultural separations, wealth gaps, the haves versus the have-nots. Patience is rare. Focus is misdirected by the loud, angry voices, and the search for peace of mind has disturbed our ability to think clearly.

Our thoughts are the food for prayer. They go hand in hand. We need both. We should never *not* want them. But what we get should be real. Patience should be in great supply, and our focus should not be on who said it but who can accomplish it.

And always remember, as it is said, "The day you plant the seed is not the day you eat the fruit."

May thoughts and prayers be with you.

Chapter 11

May Your Will Be Done

Five of the hardest words to accept in the Bible: May Your will be done.

When my pastor lost his wife, it made me wonder how he would be able to stand in front of a pulpit—or a crying mother who had a sick child, or a father on drugs who was desperate to return to life, or a teenager who felt neglected, or a single young mother whose hopes and dreams seemed dashed, or a virus plaguing the world—and say to them, "Lean on and trust in the Lord. He's in control. He'll make things right in your life and the lives of your loved ones." They watched him and his family, who are true believers—though not perfect—pray with expectation, belief, and confidence for healing in this exceptional case. After all of the work, prayers, shepherding, and leading people to Christ, they did not get what they genuinely expected—a blessing, a miracle, a testimony, healing, grace, and mercy.

How would this flock, who prayed, fasted, and believed with him and his family of faith, deal with it? How would this change their expectations when it came to our Lord and Savior Jesus Christ? How would this affect their faith, individually and collectively, being so close to the situation?

How do we not question God or face our Lord without real fear and trembling and doubt? Is this just a test or, in our minds, a

41

cruel joke? How do we raise our hands to the one who let us down and simply say, "May Your will be done"? Is that a question or a statement? Should we answer or stay quiet? Should we rejoice, cry out in disappointment, smile in acceptance, frown in confusion, get angry in pain, or simply trust and obey? The pain is real. Reality can be a beast. It's like a reoccurring dream of David and Goliath. Are we David or Goliath?

There are many stories in the Bible about those who were close to God, who walked with and even spoke to God, but suffered a bitter end for reasons only God truly knows. Trust and obey. In our small, finite minds of limited reasoning, it's no wonder that many disbelieve or fall away from the faith. This is the challenge of the true believers—to explain the unexplainable and to simply trust and obey and to allow the will of Abba Father to be done.

Take it from me—you cannot get to God by way of logic. Logic is like the gift that keeps on giving, only it turns out to be the monster that is never satisfied. Each "logical" answer only creates another question—thus, the rabbit hole. It has no beginning and no end and is as deceptive as God is unexplainable, omniscient, omnipotent, and omnipresent. The serpent attempted to deceive Eve with logic. Logic is only good if it leads you to the truth, and truth is God-breathed. Faith is absolute belief in what you can't see, know, or understand but is experienced every day. As the saying goes, life has no remote. You have to get up and change it yourself!

The Bible says that it is appointed to man once to die. Some interpret that to mean that there is a specific time, place, or date that is set for each of us to die. If there is a certain age, place, or s time appointed each person to die, does that mean that we can live any kind of way—walk out into traffic, jump off a building or bridge—and unless that is our appointed time, nothing will happen to us? Is that fate? I don't know, but it might not mean that God appoints a specific time when we will die but that God knows when we will die and that He has the last say. He can allow it or step in for reasons of His own.

There always seems to be sin behind every unnatural death though sin not always particularly of your own doing. Often it's due to unrelated sin that reaches you with no specific direct intent on hurting you. Sin is like a virus that originates in one place but spreads to many unsuspecting or underserving people. It's the COVID of spirituality. We must understand and accept that God does not have to explain His actions to us, and that can be disturbing, especially if our goal is to blindly trust and obey, to submit to the will of our Creator and Lord.

It may seem that I am building a case to not submit, more so than that of obedience, but I'm not. Reality is a dish served raw. If things were simple—if life were easy—what need would we have for a Savior? Deep down in human hearts is the reality that life has to be more than what we can see, hear, taste, feel, touch, or even think. We are too complex to have been molded out of an accidental collision of two rocks, crashing into one another in space, falling to this planet, and fusing together atoms, matter, hearts, lungs, and creative thinking, which evolved into who we are today. If there is a picture, there has to be a painter; if there is a building, there has to be a builder; if there is a creation, there has to be a creator, who has the authority and ability to do as is pleasing and true to the plan in mind.

The will of our day-to-day lives belongs to the Creator. We, the people, are not just checkers on a checkerboard but more like chess pieces on the chessboard of life, with moves that are pondered and precisely thought out, played by the Creator, who takes life seriously and adores all chess pieces. The foundation of this game, however, is the ability to predict the next move, but the Creator knows the next move in order to protect or collect the valued chess pieces.

If you now have said to yourself, "He didn't give us an answer or solution," you are right. Figure this out in whatever manner gives you peace. As for me and my house, well, Lord, may Your will be done.

Chapter 12

Blind from the Inside Out

The mind carries the body. The body offers no significant positive growth change to the mind. The body is dying, but the mind can live or has the ability to continue to grow. But it's the heart that keeps everything alive. It's that constant beating and pumping that we ignore until it skips a beat, or hurts physically or emotionally, or stops.

Truth must enter the mind before it enters the heart, which changes your soul. But the mind must be able to receive it.

> Be ye transformed by the renewing of your mind. (Romans 12:2)

And your heart must be true and good.

> The heart is deceitful above all things, and desperately wicked. (Jeremiah 17:9)

God created us as living souls and gave us bodies, through which we can experience the world around us and communicate with one another. When man fell through sin, he began to think of himself as having a soul instead of being one. A. W. Tozer said that it makes a lot of difference whether a man believes that he is a body having a soul or a soul having a body. To accept Christ stops right there, but to believe or receive Him (to hear His voice) goes on forever. He is who He is, so it is not about accepting Him. When Donald Trump was US president, no one asked us to accept him as president, but because he was president, there were problems with believing him at times.

I go to a particular yogurt store that has pictures and the names of each flavor of yogurt that they serve. They always ask me if I would like to sample anything before I buy it. They want me to believe them and receive a taste in order that I might accept it. What we do as a church is get people to "buy" it—God—before they taste or receive it. And we expect them to learn to like it before they taste it, which causes us to give them to God, instead of them choosing God for themselves.

> O taste and see that the Lord is good. (Psalm 34:8)

> ... and have tasted the good word of God and the powers of the age to come,... (Hebrews 6:5)

> If you have tasted the kindness of the Lord. (1 Peter 2:3)

> Your words were found and I ate them, and Your words became for me a joy and the delight of my heart; For I have been called by Your name, O Lord God of hosts. (Jeremiah 15:16)

The world is in a constant fight for control of our minds, our thoughts, our attention, and our money while we fight the urge to conform. We are blinded by the glamours of sin, trying to find our way out of this thick forest of options, choices, and offers of tranquility.

It is well documented that the brain is a muscle. It holds our mental thoughts, beliefs and our ability to make decisions. Because of that, it needs to be stretched, pushed and challenged to stay sharp in order to perform its intended use. Let it get sluggish and idle and that muscle will become a pitiful mass of easily influenced flab in a short period of time. Mental Health is a big deal and highly talked about subject now-a-day so allow me to make one statement about it as it pertains to Therapy. Therapy, or seeing a qualified (and preferably spiritually minded Christ centered) therapist is not an abandonment of Faith. Therapy helps to unclutter and organize your thoughts so that you can clearly hear the voice and directions of God.

Left idle, the mind will accept and believe anything that flows through it from the mouth, ears, and eyes. If you don't feed it by reading and traveling and education and the truth, it will get fat with bad thoughts, rumors, and lies, and it will develop an open-door policy that will be difficult to close. If you watch what you eat, you should also watch what you watch, validate what you hear, and monitor your thoughts. If you don't have time, then you're not managing your time wisely, based on what is important to your well-being.

Due to very little Christian representation on everyday media, except for a few hours during Sunday services, the church no longer represents mainstream Christianity in America. Like Little Red Riding Hood, we always seem to go through something bad to get to something good, and if we can't seem to see the forest for the trees, it's usually because we're too close to a tree.

Sometimes, we have to take a step back in order to keep going forward to see the fullness of what we're facing. The book of Psalms says that we are like a flower. The wind blows over it and it's gone, and its place remembers it no more. Life is like a chair; it has no favorites. If we get up, it'll accept any butt that sits on it.

Some define blindness as the inability to see outside of oneself, but there are more people blind from the inside out than from the outside in—all they can see is themselves. I've often said that we are two different people in one, who are the same. One is how we see ourselves, and the other is how others see us. They are both true; they are both one and the same person. One is our public persona; the other is our shelter-in-place person, our social-distancing person with boundaries. Some are for simple privacy; some are for distancing, hiding the pain. Ask yourself who hurt you. As you fight to release yourself, forgive those people. Then, forgive yourself. Then, change your behavior. Then, change your life. If you can't forget, then forgive—for you. Be better.

Chapter 13

Why Daddies Don't Hear You

My daughter, at an early age, would always demand my total focus on what she had to say whenever she addressed me. If you should dash away your attention for any reason—to scratch your nose or notice a Martian floating overhead—she would get upset because she wanted all of your attention focused on what she was saying—there was nothing more important than getting her point across. If she caught me glancing over at the TV in the middle of a sports game, she would accuse me of ignoring her. While I meant no disrespect, she would say, "Daddy you're not listening!"

I would then worry that she would ask me to repeat what she had said and if I missed a word, she would be very disappointed that I had not paid attention to her. If she called me while I was in the middle of a golf game, at a restaurant eating, or driving, she would always ask me if I was busy, but regardless of my answer, she would go on with her story. If my focus was interrupted by traffic, my turn to hit, or paying for my meal, she would ask, "Daddy, are you listening?" I knew I was in trouble due to my inability to focus on two or more things at the same time. At times, I missed some of her story and would ask her a question that she'd already answered, which would validate to her that I was not listening, and she would say, "Daddy, you're not listening! I told you that!" I hadn't heard her because I was focusing on something else.

When we are young, we have the ability to multitask. As we get older, multitasking diminishes to single focus or focusing on one thing at a time. That's why some people say that you didn't hear them or weren't listening to them when they talked to you, but you were simply not focusing on them, though sometimes for a split second, but on something else at that time. You don't focus on memory; you focus now on brain processing, which relates to brain exercises, such as puzzles or apps that exercise the brain or simulate brain memory, especially at an older age (April 23, 2014, "Brain neuroscience study that focused on brain memory").

I deeply respect all that my daughter says and welcome very much her conversations and the privilege of being trusted with her personal concerns. I would never intentionally disrespect that. Daddies—parents—are imperfect people trying to live up to perfect expectations.

Chapter 14

Facing Your Fears

Know that you are in the will of God. The kindness and patience of our God the Creator is something that our human minds cannot fully understand. From Job to Moses, from Esther to Joseph, Elijah and Elisha, the path taken to get to where they ended up is a mystery before our eyes but always ends in the right place at the right time. Fear's greatest allies are impatience and doubt. Timing is everything to God.

But fear is real, whether physical, financial, emotional, or any other situation that causes you to question your actions, courage, strength, self-esteem, or decision-making. Trust is an important element of overcoming fear. It's like a man walking along the bank of a raging river, and he falls in. Instead of fighting the impossible odds, he simply gives in to the flow and allows the waters to shape him, making him a part of it.

There are times in your life when for you to survive impossible odds, you must flow with the current, trusting God, not fighting, until you are given back control. Sometimes in life, holding on means letting go.

Trying to understand the mind of God outside of faith and the Bible can be challenging. Trying to understand faith also can be exhaustive and confusing. What makes you believe that you can achieve whatever goals you have in mind? What evidence do you have that is so solid that you are willing to risk, sacrifice, and go forward with what you believe or who you believe? Faith says that there is something that you know or see or feel that convinces you that what you hope for or what you want will actually come to pass. Therefore, faith shows the reality of what you hope for; it is the evidenced or things you cannot see. Faith is not a result but a motivator that moves you forward to achieve, without physical proof of anticipated results. It is blind trust with no guarantee of positive results and a chance you are willing to take. You know that failure is a possibility but *not* trying is worse than failure. You know that what you now see did not come from anything that can be seen, and you lay your trust on Him.

You see, there is no failure except that which is first created in your mind. God asks that we believe Him, regardless of the risks and in spite of the danger, ignoring the odds. If you do what He tells you and go where He leads you, the outcome will always be a victory, never a failure. Perhaps you missed the mark in your efforts because you aimed low. Yet God is merciful to those of us who deserve no mercy. Daniel 9:18 says, "We make this plea, not because we deserve help, but because of your mercy."

I once read this quote: "There is not a single saint who sits in a single church free from a few things he or she is ashamed of—not one of us! When God forgives, He forgets." Many have died with faith still dripping down their lips, but their rewards were handed to them through their trust and righteousness from God Almighty. The ultimate goal was achieved because during their journeys, by faith, to their goals, they never took their eyes off God. They also knew that theirs is a flip side of faith, where many do not achieve their goal but refuse to turn from God. They earned a good reputation because of their faith, yet none of them received all that God had promised in this life.

The reasons for fear come in many forms. Most people seek for but are afraid of Success for example. You could have so many people telling you how wonderful and successful you are that you can't see

51

who you are anymore and you lose yourself. There is nothing wrong with prosperity but prosperity can create in you a shield that causes you to become less concerned about the struggling world around you. A world that you worked hard to leave behind. While hard work is a necessary ingredient to success, the world wants you to believe that it was only that that brought you success and not the blessings of God. When you don't believe that satan exists, then you have no choice but to blame everyone else for the bad things that happens to you. That's the scary part of success. When many walk away from poverty they also walk away from their morals.

Then there is the fear of "letting go". Letting go of old memories and loved ones who have gone on to glory. How often we are reminded of our past and our mistakes, failures and words spoken out of anger and hate. Fears we can't seem to shake because of the media that punctuates our weaknesses and our history by constantly highlighting the evils in our world that peeks the public's interest and causes us to turn a blind eye and creates a scab on the heart.

Facing ones fears can be freighting and exhausting, especially when you try to face them alone. I want to mention something that seems to many people to be a blight on their reputation and that is the "T" word, Therapy. Many Christians see this as an abandonment of Faith. Therapy is not an abandonment of Faith. Therapy helps to unclutter and organize your thoughts so that you can clearly hear the voice and directions of God. In my opinion, Therapy must be done with someone who is reputable, wise, open and honest about life in general and spiritually based in particular. Therapy can be done with a professional therapist or with and accompanied by a legal and moral act or hobby that calms your spirit such as soothing and calming music, art or running. Writing for me is therapeutic.

Fear is a battle. Battles are not always designed to be won; they are designed to teach you how to survive. Wars are made to be won. You go to boot camp to learn how to survive the battle; you go through battles to learn how to win the war. So count it all as joy when you go through—when you make it through—the boot camp trials. The true battle for us is between good and evil. There is only one war, and God has already won that by way of Christ Jesus, our Lord and Savior. Preachers are called to teach survival skills.

When a third of God's angels revolted against their Creator, God kicked them down to this empty void of a rock now called Earth. This was Satan's kingdom. Those angels were created separately, and they are not family or related. On this same rock God chose to build His family, in the middle of Satan's kingdom, starting with Adam and Eve. His family was created on the same rock as the opposing enemy. Should you expect this to be a battleground or a playground? Too many Christians have gotten so comfortable in this world that they have little desire to leave it.

If you are on a boat in the middle of a raging river, and you try to play chess, there are gonna be problems. If you try to light a candle, there are gonna be problems. If you try to put on makeup, there are gonna be problems. The problems are there because you are on a raging river—a battleground, not a playground—so expect problems instead of getting upset because the ground is shaking. Don't look for a way to stop the problem; find a way to resolve the problem. If you stop it, it's still there, waiting; if you resolve it, it's gone. Look to your source, not your resource.

An objective lesson of life is this: The bias of nature is toward the wilderness, never toward the fruitful field—spiritually and materially. If left unattended, things get worse instead of better. Fruit rots with time instead of ripening. Prepared grounds bend toward the wilderness if not kept up. Humanity gets older and weaker instead of younger and stronger (but not of the spirit). What is true of the ground is true of the soul. If left unattended, it too will dissipate to its most egregious state, challenging and confronting our spirits. The acceptance of Christ does not guarantee a victorious, prosperous and fruitful living for the rest of your days on earth, only goodness and mercy (Psalm 23:6).

Like a garden, you must constantly cultivate and attend it. Neglect it, and the wilderness will relentlessly seek to take back what has been taken from it. So is the moral bent of a fallen world, as the temptation of this world fights to win back what it has lost. This is the battleground. Adam and Eve's playground has now turned into a battleground because that is what neglect and disobedience does.

We are like a ball in a pinball machine at times, where we simply roll until we hit something. No plan, no goal, no real future. Just roll with the punches. That's no way to live! The greater part of you is on the inside, and that beating sound you hear in your chest may not be your heart but the better part of you trying to get out! Listen from the inside out.

There are times in your life when, to survive impossible odds, you must flow with the current, trusting God, not fighting it, until you are able to regain control. The lifting up of your head is found in knowing that God has your back. Know that whatever is happening in your life is not without God's knowledge. I said this once but I think it bears repeating. Facing your fears and knowing that you are in the will of God changes everything! Knowing that we are in the will of God changes everything. Nothing intimidates those who know that what they believe is based on what God has said. It allows them to stand strong and confident! Know that you are in the will of God!

Chapter 15

Don't Follow the Leader; Lead the Followers

There was a commercial on TV once in which children are in a swimming pool, playing a game called Marco Polo. The camera then panned over to show that Marco Polo himself was actually in the pool with them—he raised his arms, saying, "Excuse me, I am here!"—but they never recognized him or even saw that he was in the pool.

We're human, and humans live off bursts of emotions that flare up with a bright and exciting light but quickly fade away. We wait on the next explosion, having forgotten the last one as quickly as it faded away. We follow, live for, and placate other human beings, with a little Jesus on the side.

Don't follow the leader; lead the followers! Always determine a path to follow.

Your path determines your target. Satan is not here to change your mind; he's here to change your thinking. One is temporary (mind); the other is forever (thinking). It's not to change your brain but to change your heart, and not all at once but progressively, one lie at a time. One "This is how I grew up in the hood" at a time. One "this is all I ever knew" at a time. One bad relationship, one bad parent, one cigarette, one joint, one baby daddy, one baby mama at a time.

After he's infiltrated your mind and your thinking, he can let you go on your own because he's got you where he wants you and has other minds to destroy. If he infiltrates your thoughts and leads you the wrong way, he can train your actions. Why is Satan so persistent, so determined, so desperate, so hurried? I believe the answer is in his name—SATAN, which stands for "Such a Time as Now." All he has is *now* because when now ends, eternity begins.

Don't be led. Lead!

Chapter 16

White Privilege, Black Opportunity

White privilege is so pervasive now that many of those who are privileged to take advantage of it are not doing it intentionally. The perception of white privilege is so ingrained that it is more of a reaction than an intentional act. White privilege is systemic. White privilege is an ingrained, untrue bias on white people.

White privilege created racism. The continued efforts of white people to hold on to it has created a moral monster in their hearts and souls, for those who fit this definition. It is real, no matter how much you deny it. It is part of reality, a moral dilemma. It is now so woven into the fabric of white America that it is mostly a common reaction rather than a purposeful action. Many white people do not walk into an establishment, flashing their white privilege card. And no reasonable person will turn down an accepted opportunity that is sought, regardless of the underlying reason of privilege.

White superiority and white privilege are ingrained perceptions now. To too many, it is as real as flesh. White people are not comfortable with the inevitability of their past and are certainly not willing to give up their place in line. You cannot change that perception by any other principle of force, marching, violence,

destruction of person or property, or new laws, thinking that your
will change the mind of man, white or otherwise.

> Be ye transformed by the renewing of your mind.
> (Romans 12:2)

It is not the mind that must change. A transformed mind
changes the heart from deceitful and desperately wicked (Jeremiah
17:9) to honest and compassionate caring. Truth must enter the
mind before it enters the heart, but the mind must be able to receive
it. No race has to do twice as much or be twice as good as any
other race to receive respect and proper due. Nor does being "color
blind" make you any different from those who see and reject color.
You can't be "woke" in black-and-white and dream in color. That's
the strange thing about racism—it's not about race (there are white
African Americans), or religion (there are black Jews and people of
all religions), or sexuality (male or female matters not), or status (rich
and poor come in all races). It's about color—the color of one's skin.

James Baldwin, author of *I Am Not Your Negro*, did not see the
black problem as racism but as a moral problem, deep in the heart
of white America. He said that the root of the black man's hatred is
rage. He doesn't so much hate the white man; he just simply wants
him out of the way—and more than that, out of his children's way.
He also says that the root of the white man's hatred (those who do)
is terror. This problem within them that they invented, which fights
within them to safeguard their purity and position, has created a
monster within them (some, not all), and it is destroying them.

It's what's in the hearts of some people that slowly infects their
moral fiber and changes the heart of man. Perhaps this is what Martin
Luther King Jr. saw that moved him to fight for his nonviolent stand.
The problem was not in the actions of white people, but in the
hearts of white people. No amount of force can change the heart.
This, in a strange way, made Dr. King feel more compassion for
white people whose hearts were infected by this "moral disease." He

saw people from the inside out, as opposed to from the outside in. For others, such as Malcolm X, that was a hard pill to swallow, and understandably so. One will always attack what one sees.

There is but one institution whose sole purpose is to change the heart of man and that can make that change in the heart of man. That institution is the church, a power beyond the mind and heart of man, and that power belongs to God by way of Jesus and the Holy Spirit. The church is not a solution that many want to hear because it relies on your giving up some control of your decisions. It also exposes your faults, denials, personal feelings, and prejudices for others to see—and even worse, for you to see.

People don't seem to care about life, liberty, and the pursuit of happiness. What they care about is their lives, their liberty, and *their* pursuit of happiness. That's the new world that we now live in. It's no longer about morality but about the Constitution now. The Constitution now trumps morality. It's not what God wants; it's what the people want.

Generation to generation, people are becoming more sensitive and more emotional. Actions, past events, or lack of self-esteem or acceptance easily trigger unrestrained emotions, (physically and mentally) and a lack of self-control. We either have to change with them, adjust to them, or fall because of them. Sometimes we are so busy trying to be who we want to be or who others want or expect us to be that we fail to see who we really are. There are things that all races can teach each other. We're not going to get it if we constantly demand commonalities without accepting our differences and don't face our past—good, bad, and ugly.

Everyone is dealt a hand in this poker game of life. Stop peeking at the hand next to you, and start concentrating on the hand dealt to you, and plan your next move. While white people do have a privileged advantage, is the true advantage in being white, or is it who's taking advantage of whatever opportunity you may have generationally? Would the results had been any different if the little boy in the Bible had one fish and two loaves? The goal will always be the same. The level of commitment that it takes to do extraordinary things is usually not ordinary. Make it work! The one who starts the ball rolling owns the ball.

CNN.com reported in an article by Matt Egan, CNN Business on January 26, 2021, that America's billionaires grew $1.1 trillion richer during the coronavirus pandemic. There are 614 billionaires in the United States, and only seven of them are black, according to the Insider – Business News & More on buinessinsider.com dated Sep. 4, 2020 by Taylor Nicole Rogers. There are only 13 to 15 in the entire world depending on various CNN and other news reports as they are constantly changing.

In my opinion it seems that the stock market has played a significant role in the divide between rich and poor. Not surprisingly, surging stock prices are especially helpful to the wealthy because they have more skin in the game. The report stated that it will take more than a decade for the world's poorest to recoup their losses from the pandemic, according to Oxfam International's annual inequality report. By contrast, it took just nine months for the world's top one thousand billionaires to recover.

I don't mean to suggest that money is black and brown people's biggest problem. Realistically, money is only a resource, not a source, and resources run out. It is building and maintaining the machine that makes the money, and that machine is the biggest problem in our culture now. The machine I'm referring to is composed of God, family, and education, in that order. It's like the old adage of baking a cake. You need butter and flour and milk. When asked how to bake a cake, however, you don't say, "Pour the batter in the pan and put it in the oven." You must be able to explain the ingredients that made up the batter.

We must be able to step back and break down the ingredients that make up the black culture and identify the ingredient that caused the cake to fall. If we can't change the culture, then we must change ourselves. I think we are at that point where we have to change us—our plan, our thinking, our priorities. No one's going to give us a free ride—not that we're asking for one, nor is white America willing to step out of the place that they are in now.

Galatians 5:7 says, "Who stepped in front of you during your race and interrupted your run?"

So tell yourself, "You were running a good race. Who cut in on you, keeping you from obeying and facing the truth?"

Chapter 17

Do Black Lives (Really) Matter?

The Black Lives Matter movement is pervasive nowadays. Yes, all lives matter, but humanity usually focuses on the least of these—the hurting, the less fortunate, the ones left behind, the squeakiest wheel, the ones who cause the scales not to balance. Blacks seem to fall into one or more of those categories for one reason or another. I'll not get into the initial origin of Black Lives Matter—you should investigate that for yourself, as it was not initially a slogan meant for what it now stands for. But since it has taken the mantra of the need for equality and fairness for black people, I want to speak on what I think its deeper meaning should be, as opposed to what its surface meaning is. As a black man, I think I at least have the right to comment on it.

Black Lives Matter *should not* be a narrative shouted out to white folks that our black lives matter. Black Lives Matter should be a commitment, a message from us to us, that our lives matter because the uplifting of our people will first have to come from and be done with black hands. I should also say not to expect something from others that you can't give to yourself—things like respect and honor, clean communities, superior education, proper raising of our children, accountability for our own actions, and being prepared for what we are marching and shouting for. Individually and collectively, we must ask ourselves, "Are we whole enough to accept or take care of and preserve that for which we are asking?" Would you know what to do with forty acres and a mule, or, in the end, would your children end up with one acre and a dog?

We must focus on the need to give our children a sense of responsibility and accountability or they will destroy the positive work done and progress made. Not only will they be handed what we fought and died for, but our actions will influence the decisions of future generations on *how* to maintain and not *sink back* and destroy the positive work done and progress made. It not only affects them but allows them to face the consequences of their bad choices financially, educationally, and spiritually.

We must stop comparing ourselves to and competing with white people and turn our focus onto what we are doing to ourselves.

> Pay careful attention to your own work, for then you will get the satisfaction of a job well done, and you won't need to compare yourself to anyone else. For we are each responsible for our own conduct. (Galatians 6:4–5)

In Payton Manning's Hall of Fame speech, he said something that made me think, and it allowed me to take a peek into the mind of someone whose family is generationally successful, both on and off the field. I'll tweak what he said to apply it to us.

> Our legacy is only worthwhile when there's a future to fuel. While we can ignite the fire, future generations (our children) must fan the flames.

It is no longer only about our present generation; it's about surviving and preparing for another day, year, and decade and generations to come, and that doesn't come without focus, planning, sacrifice, and hard work. We, as a people, got a little too relaxed after laws were passed, constitutions made, and amendments ratified in writing but not in the hearts of men.

This is about stepping around those who stand in our way and standing beside those who stand with us. This is about not allowing anger, envy, or revenge to cut in front of us in our race to our goals. It's about not being distracted by fear, name-calling, failure, or those who expect us to fall. It's about teaching the next generation how to fish and not simply how to be fed; how to become owners and not borrowers or renters; how to be accountable to our own actions and decisions because you can't depend on people who depend on you, especially when they are at an age when they should be independent.

A lot of our children are a reflection of the training—or lack thereof—of their parents, who themselves may not have had adequate training, but somewhere in that race for intelligence, accountability and common sense has to kick in.

It is no secret, yet it's a disgrace, that we have faltered and wobbled due to the irresponsibility and lack of accountability of too many of our black men. Our neglect comes by way of irresponsible fathers, illegitimate dads and coping with life's difficulties in destructive ways. Drugs use, sex, and a lack of proper morals are destructive ways being used in order to be and stay in control while believing that this behavior will give him the respect and honor he feels is due him. It is also not a secret that black women are losing the respect and honor due our black men and have carved a path for themselves without them. And, it doesn't help that our country is acquiescing to the legalization of the very drugs, gun laws and racial fears that have become the very triggers that affect the black and brown population and contributes to the poverty, incarceration and present day family structure.

While these assessments don't apply to all black men or women, there is beginning to be too many to separate.

What will it take to turn the ship? I don't know for sure, but I can give my suggestions on a good place to start. It's gonna take teachers to teach well, lawyers to protect our rights, and politicians with a heart for people. If preachers, our greatest influencers, are going to make a difference in the future of this world, they will have to make that difference with those who will be our future—our youth. You need to listen to their music, you need to listen to their conversations, and you need to get your shoes a little dirty and get out of those pulpits and into the pit. You must be physically and mentally ready to move when God says go! But in true confessions, who am I to tell a called man of God what he should or should not be doing?

> For God has not given us a spirit of fear and timidity,
> but of power, love and self-discipline.
> (2 Timothy 1:7 NLT)

If God didn't give us fear and timidity, we must have gotten it from human sources. Job 12: 12 says, "Wisdom belongs to the aged, and understanding to the old." We must also read more, which provides us with infinite information; travel more, which opens the mind to possibilities and removes the stigma of limitations; and plan because budgeting and focusing on our goals allow dreams to become reality. Lastly, we must understand before we take a stand. We must conquer our fears but replace them with wisdom, and that wisdom must not stay dormant but must be passed on.

We must stop bouncing around with no objective nor plan for our future and live with a purpose. Yes, be content but never satisfied. There is no failure except that which is first created in our minds. God asks that we believe Him, regardless of the risks, in spite of the danger, and ignoring the odds while fighting off the naysayers. Through Him, we must silent the accusers within us.

As I've said previously and is worth repeating, if you do what God tells you and go where He leads you, the outcome will always be a victory, never a failure. We may lose many battles, but we are out to win the war. Aim higher!

Our struggle is indeed our strength. I'll say again that Black Lives Matter should represent a commitment to make the lives of black folks "matter" by making their lives better, and this needs to start with black hands. It is not a statement that says that black lives matter only today; it's a statement that says we will make our lives matter going forward, and that takes planning and preparation and moral thinking before we act.

It should matter more within our community and not as much outside of our community, where we lose our true focus. We should trade reparation for preparation. One has diminishing qualities, while the other goes on forever, generation to generation. Much time and much sacrifice will be needed. How much do you want it? We cannot exceed the expectations of those outside of our race until we exceed the expectations within our own race.

Chapter 18

Confronting Your Deepest Personal Need

People who do the things that they do—such as protest marching that results in destruction of property, coming out as gay, or exhibiting racial hatred—don't always do those things because of the issue at hand but because of a lack of significance in their personal lives. These acts of indifference, hatred, aggression, destruction, well-meaning intent, and protesting give them the attention and power they crave, even as part of a group, and give them significance, payback, or the relief of guilt and an excusable purpose that they sorely lack in their personal lives, along with their drive for change and acceptance.

These personal issues are as real as the issues they are fighting for and acting out. To quash this action, one must find out what their deepest personal need is and provide real answers. Their environmental and survival needs may be a reminder of a more painful personal need—a feeling of inadequacy or lack of significance. People need to be reminded that God has provided every person with significance and a meaningful purpose for their lives, and they are really searching for that meaning. Destructive thoughts and behavior are just that, DESTRUCTIVE. To fight destructive behavior with destructive behavior is, YES, destructive and solves nothing.

We must also understand and accept that God doesn't have a wonderful plan for everybody's life here on this planet, even though He has a purpose for every person who believes in and receives Him. For some, His plan is to accept; for others, His plan is to deny. Mark Twain once said that the two most important days in a person's life are the day he is born and the day he finds out why.

It is dreadful to go through life without a purpose outside of yourself. Maybe we only need to be pointed in the right direction that leads to the answer.

Chapter 19

Mind the Gap

While riding the subways in London, the one thing I heard over the microphone to the herds of people getting on and off the train was, "Mind the gap." It didn't take long to figure out what that statement meant. It was a warning. There is a gap between the train platform and the train floor as you enter and exit the train through the automatic doors. If you were to get your foot caught in that space, or gap, you most likely would lose a foot, if not your life. The message was that there is always a small danger that creates a big problem if you don't stay focused on your task at hand, stay alert to your surroundings, and mind the little things.

I wrote a personal unpublished booklet, titled *Beware of the Locust*, in 2006 that I gave away to people who were going through troubled times due to sickness, death of a loved one, depression, or a low point in their lives. This was my attempt to give them some perspective in a time when they needed to bear life's burdens. It was a warning, a statement that echoed through the halls of despair by people caught in the snares of the unfortunate and unexpected circumstances of life—the gap. It's the space between where you are coming from and where you are going, the place that represents more than we can bear.

Mind the gap, to me, was a reminder to those whose minds were on so many things that it distorted their focus on what was in front of them. Before you get to where you are going, there are gaps of danger, trouble, and unforeseen but small perils of life that, while seemingly minimal, must be given peripheral attention to avoid major issues in life. This may sound trivial, until it happens to you. Mind the gap!

Chapter 20

The Trivial Pursuit of Happiness vs. the Desperate Retreat from Sadness

How important is being happy, whatever that is for you? How critical is it to your right to life? How much effort should you put in to being happy? The US Constitution guarantees life, liberty and the "pursuit" of happiness. Is the work that we put into avoiding sadness also counted as the act of pursuing happiness, or are we setting ourselves up for a fall from which we may never be able to recover? Perhaps the pursuit of happiness is simply a desperate retreat from sadness. Maybe that is why in the minds of many the pursuit for a normal, happy life in America for some seems so "trivial". The fight for what is rightfully yours becomes exhausting. Happiness is not offered in the US Constitution nor is it a given right but the *pursuit* of happiness is.

I was reading a summary of a book titled *Grit*, written by Angela Duckworth, in which she described her attempt to find out why many high achievers who were selected for the final list of candidates for the prestigious West Point Academy dropped out of training or lost interest "before they could realize their potential," after they'd put in such hard work to get there. She noted an interesting realization—in a deep sense, none of the cadets believed they would ever reach their highest expectations, but all were addicted to the chase, the enduring passion and determination of the "pursuit," as much as the capture. The process was as motivating to them as was the goal. It was the combination of passion and perseverance that made high achievers successful. If you can't deal with what it takes to get to your dreams or pursuits, failure is imminent.

The book of Ecclesiastes is a very interesting read. In Chapter 1:1-8 It talks about the pointless pursuit of acquiring things in life that are supposed to make us happy, but, in the end, it turns out to be a consuming chase after the wind. King Solomon wrote:

> In my opinion, nothing is worthwhile; everything is futile. For what does a man get for all his hard work? Generations come and go but it makes no difference. The sun rises and sets and hurries around to rise again. The wind blows south and north, here and there, twisting back and forth, getting nowhere. The rivers run into the sea but the sea is never full, and the water returns again to the rivers, and flows again to the sea ... everything is unutterably weary and tiresome. No matter how much we hear, we are not content.

Another interesting point made by Solomon is this (Eccl. 2:18-25):

> And I am disgusted about this, that I must leave the fruits of all my hard work to others. And who can tell whether my son will be a wise man or a fool? And yet all I have will be given to him—how discouraging!

I can just imagine that Solomon wrote that after a long day of pursuing happiness while turning his back on the sadness that lagged just behind him. He likely was tired of the ups and downs of life and realized, after a while, that all that he had done and all that he could do had been done before. Happiness was like cotton candy—sweet, fluffy sugar that melted as soon as it touched your tongue, while your taste buds called out for more.

We try to blot out the sound of the hoofbeats of time and age as they get louder and louder, but alas, time is and always will be undefeated. So what does old Solomon conclude in this dilemma, this war between happiness and sadness, that humans face?

> So I conclude that, first, there is nothing better for a man than to be happy and to enjoy himself as long as he can; and second, that he should eat and drink and enjoy the fruits of his labor, for these are gifts from God. (Ecclesiastes 3:12–13)

I'll conclude this chapter with more thoughts from Solomon:

> When the clouds are heavy, the rains come down; when a tree falls, whether south or north, the die is cast, for there it lies. If you wait for perfect conditions, you will never get anything done. God's ways are as mysterious as the pathway of the wind, and as the manner in which a human spirit is infused into the little body of a baby while it is yet in its mother's womb. Keep on sowing your seed, for you never know which will grow—perhaps it all will. It is a wonderful thing to be alive! (Ecclesiastes 11:3–8)

No one is responsible for your happiness but you.

Be responsible for your actions, and always try to do what is right and good. When you fall, fall forward, then extend your hand to accept help, and then reach your hand down to give help.

Lastly, the three corners of the triangle of life that will almost guarantee you success in life are as follows:

1. A Structured Life

Focus on having a balanced life. Repetition is not bad or boring but consistent. In some things, you should know what to expect.

Stability is an important part of a grounded life. It helps you care about someone other than yourself. Prioritize family, and value strong relationships. Fight the urge to conform.

2. Actions over Words

In 2 Corinthians 10:10, Paul mentioned, in one of his letters to the Corinthians, that he had heard that his letters were thought to be "strong and bold" but that he, in person, was weak and feeble. His comeback was that while he might be strong in word and weak in person, he was always strong in action.

One of the lessons in that is to not give your word if you can't keep it. Think and plan over action and words. Preparation is the key. Don't complain; do something. While words have value in some cases, in other cases, they are worthless. Give back, if you are blessed to do so, while looking forward. There's always somebody in need.

3. Strong Faith—Moral Center

Your needs will always be based on your knees. May we stop exploiting God in the name of love so that we may have our way over His. May we recognize and stop influencers of lies and deceit, who are blinded by the glamor of sin, acceptance, prosperity, praise, or popularity. The gospel is the adoption and acceptance of a nonnegotiable, nonevolving lifestyle, based on the life and standard of Jesus Christ; it's not a way of life that is based on your thoughts, desires, or beliefs. Love is birthed from this lifestyle, not as the result of it.

You are never as bad as you or others think you are, nor are you as good as you or others think you are. Accept your mistakes, ask for forgiveness, and always try to unselfishly put yourself in position for the next step in life that God may have for you. Never beat yourself up for mistakes or carry them with you; give them to the Lord, inhale deeply, exhale, and then move on!

Chapter 21

I Don't Want What You Have; I Want You

I inherited from my mom her need and dependency on God. She was proof to me that you'll never see what you don't look for, and you'll never question what you don't ask. Her purpose in my life was clear.

Many people close to you—in your family, in your world environment, in your circle of friends, in your network, in your life, Twitter or Instagram followers—may be a part of your life but are not a part of God's plan for you. Many are there only for that particular time and place in your life.

The arguments and ended relationships for which we beat ourselves up are not our fault. There are and will be many things that we should never have let into our hearts that must now be broken out to be released. And that can sometimes be a hard pill to swallow or accept or even recover from; it's something you may never understand or fully get over without a lot of faith and a little amnesia.

We were created with an incorruptible body. Then the body was corrupted by sin, much like the COVID-19 virus. The virus cannot be spoken away or forgiven; it must be destroyed. Once you are infected with the virus (of sin), you become highly infectious around people because there is a very real chance that you will infect all with whom you come in contact, much like the virus of sin. Someone must first acquire this virus and that person or entity that holds that disease (sin) cannot be forgiven but must find a vaccine that will fight it within your body. We let some of these diseases into our hearts voluntarily but unknowingly and with seemingly no symptoms. We often determine the value of something or someone based on how they make us feel, not based on their needs.

Your thanks and compliments to them are statements of how they made you feel, with very little personal sacrifice from you. Perhaps, because of sin, we can't be trusted to stay on course and in our lane, according to God's will and plan for our lives. We are vulnerable, easily tempted, and drawn off course by our own thinking. While trust is critical, sometimes you have to love a person enough to not trust them.

Don't confuse love with trust. They are two separate, distinct, and different realities that depend on one another but often let each other down. Our dependency on one another weakens our dependency on God. People, especially our youth, don't want to hear what you say; they want to see what you're doing. One of our biggest societal problems is that we teach our children how to be successful, but we fail to teach them how to fail. That sounds contrary to forward thinking or forward progress, doesn't it? Kind of like learning to hit down on a golf ball in order for the ball to go up.

My message to you is this:

You can stick your finger in the ocean and move the water around with ease. Yet a 60,000-ton ship floats on that water, regardless of how big or how heavy it is. No matter how high the waves or how tumultuous the winds may blow and batter against that ship, a ship will only sink when the water outside of it gets inside of it.

Life is like that ship. The water all around us is life's problem. We are the ships, and while the winds batter us regularly and the waves rock us constantly, we will not sink unless we allow that which is around us—the negative outside forces (waters) of life—to penetrate us and get inside. We must continually batten down the hatches of our lives and always be prepared for the turbulent waters of the world around us.

> I am coming to you for the third time, and I will not be a burden to you. I don't want what you have—I want you. After all, children don't provide for their parents. Rather, parents provide for their children. (2 Corinthians 12:14)

I will come to you for as many times as is necessary, and my hope is not to be a burden to you but to show you my love for you—to shield you, to protect you. My purpose in this time, in this place, is to provide for you, to keep the boat steady until my time is up.

Chapter 22

Blind by Birth—the Science of Thought

I'd like to share a comment I read in one of the many writings and sermons from Pastor Charles Swindoll. My added thoughts are in brackets:

> Because we have an enemy we cannot see does not mean he is not real. [This alone reminded me that we also have a God that we cannot see.]
>
> There are trials we endure that we don't deserve, but they are permitted. [These are trials, not punishments. Don't get them confused! Trials are lessons with the purpose of making us better—boot camp experiences. Punishments are the results of disobedience.] Life includes trials that we do not deserve, but they must nevertheless be endured. In the book of Job 2:3, God says to Satan about Job, "Even though you urged me to harm him without cause." In the mystery of God's unfathomable will, there are elements we can never explain or fully understand. Don't try to grasp each thread of His profound plan. If you do, you'll become

increasingly more confused, ultimately resentful, and finally bitter. Accept it. Endure the trial that has been permitted by God. Job did nothing to deserve what happened to him yet at the end he praised God because he knew that all he had was on loan. Nothing belongs to any of us, not our possessions, our children, not even our own lives. God allowed these catastrophes to happen. Nothing touches your life that has not first passed through the hand of God. He is in full control, and because He is, He has the sovereign right to permit trials that we don't deserve.

There are many things in this world that we cannot see or understand; there is much confusion and misunderstanding. God's Word says that it's not them; it's you. The world says it's not you; it's them. People change from the inside out, not the outside in. An objective lesson of life is that it is said by A.W.Tozer "The Hunger of The Wilderness", "The bias of nature is toward the wilderness, never towards the fruitful field … and what is true of the field is true of the soul."

A. W. Tozer also said in this book:

> The natural man must know in order to believe;
> But the spiritual man must believe in order to know.
> The faith that saves is not a conclusion drawn from evidence.

Faith is not a cure. It is the accelerant of the truth. That's why science gives no credit to God, when science is the very evidence of the existence of God. While science has shown its value in humanity, it is not our savior. During this COVID crisis, science has seemingly stepped into the place of God. If science is so great, why can't it prove or disprove the existence of God? While science can be a resource, it should never be a substitute for our source, God Almighty. Why? Because science is the evidence of the existence of God.

The disproval of anything only validates the existence of that which is disproven, for it has to exist before being proven as nonexistent. Existence starts with a belief in the mind, which is intangible and physically untouchable. Science requires the existence of something physical, tangible, and touchable to prove that it does or doesn't exist. I'm not saying that science is not credible; I'm just saying to give credit where credit is due. Belief starts in the mind before it finds its home in the heart. That's why faith is the evidence of things *unseen*.

A cure is not what humanity needs. Change is what humanity needs, and the change has to come from the inside out. Religion assumes that humanity can change—that if you can move one way, you have the ability to turn around and go the other way or in a new direction. Those who seek religion seek change. They feel a deviation from the norm, whatever that is to each, but they have no real example of what the norm is.

So we search for what makes us feel good and whole—something that we can touch, see, or feel as evidence of its existence. We refuse to accept that what we do is who we are, that it's not a misdirected lifestyle we live; it's a flaw within us, within our souls. COVID and other outside forces are just warnings of that need for change. It's much like the burning bush that Moses saw, as described in the Bible. Its purpose is to create the unusual in order to get our attention.

God's angel never spoke to Moses from that burning bush until Moses responded to the bush, focused on it, and walked toward it. One can be blind and see, and one can see and still be blind. Thinking does not require sight.

Chapter 23

The Subliminal Language of Change

I perceive that there is a subliminal changing of human thought and belief through false repetitious language that is permeating our culture and has been for decades, if not throughout time. Sort of like someone choking on a sip of beverage and saying that it "went down the wrong pipe," when there's only one pipe, thus causing people to think that there are two "pipes" in the human throat. If repeated enough times, an untruth becomes truth without the need to investigate or validate. Repetition breeds belief, false or otherwise, which makes one wonder why we fight so fervently against the truth and so quickly accept an unproven statement.

"God only helps those who help themselves." Really? We've gone from referring to the *father (or mother) of my child* to *my baby daddy* (or *baby mama*). Terminology has changed from *dope* to *illegal substance*; from *queer* to *homosexual* to *gay* to *the gay community* to *the trans community* to LGBT; from *created as man or woman* to *those who identify as ...*; from *abortion* to *pro-choice* or *pro-life*; from *the Creator* to *God* to *the man upstairs* or *woman upstairs* to *Him or Her* in conversations and now in science. The biblical mandate of man as head of house and family has become a cry for equality. We've gone from a conversation, to rap music, texting, and now even sexting!

Stop the madness! Beware of the influencers of this world who are slowly and methodically changing the dynamics and the very definitions and existence of normalcy by wanting to cross over and even erase proper lanes to blur the notion of an absolute standard. We often can be so influenced by the things that we are used to doing that we don't recognize the right thing or better thing when we see it, nor can we recognize or accept the need to change. Influencers' greatest weapon is repetition turned to reality until it becomes the "normal" thing to do.

I love television and radio commercials. They are short, text versions of life in its truest sense. No room for fluff, just the facts—though they often are manipulated to a subliminal message that the gullible absorb. There was, for example, a TV commercial that portrayed a cute, excitable, and happy dog, playing with a stick that was thrown by its owner. The owner went shopping to find an object to throw that was more appropriate than an old stick for the dog to fetch, and he found just the thing—a baseball-sized, multicolored, soft, fluffy ball. He took it back to his dog and hid it behind his back to surprise his best friend, who sat in obedience in front of him, wagging his tail while waiting on the surprise. His owner brought it out, waved it around to arouse his dog's excitement, and then threw it for the dog to fetch.

After a few seconds, the dog came back—with a stick. You see, the dog had been trained and influenced through repetition and praise to think that the stick made his master happy.

Commercials are a huge tool for subliminal change. For example, when I hear the music used in a commercial aimed at young people, I often try to find the original song from which the commercial's music was taken—only to find the uncut original version is full of profanity, lewdness, and sexual and racial language and suggestions. While the older generation may not be familiar with the song or its composer, the young folks recognize it immediately, with the temptation to play it when they are away from those who despise it.

My message? Please stay away from the forces of influence and influencers that can smear your road to success. Be open-minded, be smart, and be careful. Life's roads are camouflaged with one-way signs that can steer you away from being the best you can be. Don't be like everybody else. Be the best version of you. Be the version of you that you would be willing to show God. You won't regret it.

Chapter 24

Perspective: The Dirty Truth about the Divided States of America

There is one act that goes unappreciated these days. That is the private act of wiping your own butt. If someone else does this act for you, it's probably not because you are wealthy, famous, or important but because you are unable to do it for yourself. Then, you will then appreciate it and yearn to do it.

In the Bible (John 11:42), Lazarus was sacrificed and raised "for the benefit of those standing around." He was one man brought back to life for the benefit of many. Lazarus was in a better place before he was called back, only to die again for the benefit of those there who were given the chance to see, believe, and receive Christ.

The vaccine for COVID-19 only benefits those who believe that the virus is real. Those who believe in it will take it for the benefit of those who don't believe in order to save many. Still, many will not believe, but for the benefit of those who will … "I'm going to take the vaccine shot!"

> These are the promises that enable you to share his divine nature and escape the world's corruption caused by human desires. (2 Peter 1:4)

> The temptations in your life are no different from
> what others experience. ... When you are tempted,
> He will show you a way out so that you can endure.
> (1 Cor. 10:13)

Our choices cause the world's corruptions—problems. Perhaps the question is not, "Why can't you?" but "Why won't you?" This is not a guilt trip. It shows how deeply rooted sin is in the now-corrupted human body and the believing, thinking mind.

Though there are many variations of definitions, Encyclopedia Britannica's definition of Science is "the intellectual and practical activity encompassing the systematic study of the structure and behavior of the physical and natural world through observation and experiment." It is the study of how we react to certain situations in order that we may copy those acceptable reactions and maintain our present lifestyles—to see and attempt to replicate God. That is not to say that we should not use the scientific intellect that God has given us, but we should not to leave God out.

The United States hangs its hat on a thing called "rights." Most things are evaluated based on whether or not one has the legal right to do or say something. Rights are human privileges.

God gave the Ten Commandments, however, not the Ten Rights. Rights must be filtered through God's commandments, and if they don't adhere to God's standards, God's commands should take precedence. God's commands override any rights or any court decisions. A court judge or any official cannot override what they swear their oath by, which is the Bible; if so, it renders the law null and void. So before you say that you have the right to do something, filter it first through God's command.

Doctors evaluate, operate, and prescribe, but God heals. Farmers cultivate, plant, and harvest, but God grows. Police are called, and they investigate and apprehend, but God protects. Presidents oversee laws, render decisions for the benefit of the people, and cultivate peaceful existence between nations, but God rules.

Chapter 25

Stuck on Happy

When you are young, your mind is stuck on happy. As you grow older, your mind shifts to joy.

Many people believe that it is in our creative DNA to be happy. There is no obligation for happiness in this now-diluted and sin-infected world, though it is something that we all want and have come to expect.

I don't mean that we are to expect a life of pain, depression, sorrow, and misery or that we have nothing to be proud of, being poor and pitiful. We are asked to trust and to be content and to embrace joy. These are the veined roots of happiness that are buried deep into the ground of the soul. They are untouchable and can't be plucked off of your tree of life by just anyone or given away without your permission. You can either be happy or unhappy, but there is no such thing as joy or "unjoy."

We read in the Bible that throughout Jesus's life, there were no periods of self-happiness that were important enough for God to include in His sixty-six books—no visiting the happy side of kid Jesus swinging on a makeshift swing, swimming in a pond with friends, or blowing out candles at His birthday party, not even at the celebration where He turned the water into wine or at His Last Supper with His disciples.

Some people are simply put here for a specific reason at a specific time and place, and being happy in their lives escapes them because their purpose was more important than their happiness. While both can be had, their crown was joy.

Happiness is normally measured by the paths of our lives. Read the book of Solomon, or Proverbs, or the book of Ecclesiastes. Trust in the Lord with joy, and let Him direct your path. An unauthored, shock value, mythical statement I once heard in a public conversation defined the repetition of 'bad behavior' as "selling stupid". So seek happiness, expect joy, and stop "selling stupid".

Chapter 26

Humpty-Dumpty Has Fallen

As stated earlier, the United States of America is swiftly changing into the Divided States of America. Our country, our world, continues to break away and drift apart like islands. It's not just divided between blacks and whites, or the have and have-nots, or the poor and wealthy, or Democrats and Republicans; it's also divided between those who want and those who don't want, those who care and those who don't care, those who reach out for the future and those who don't, those who value life and those who don't, those who understand one another and those who don't care to understand, those who try and those who have simply given up—and, sadly, those who believe in God and the works of Christ and those who no longer reach for or believe there is a lifeboat. There is no treatment, pill, or amount of therapy that can salvage such a made-up mind. It's your choice. God will not force you into His lifeboat. You must "choose ye this day." (Josh. 24:15)

> While I learn my lessons each day,
> Allow me to give some of my life away.
> To help, not to impede,
> Those who are in need. (DSWalker)

We are slowly drifting away from our purpose and quickly drifting out of our lanes. The women's movement is shifting the family hierarchy. Technology is destroying human contact. Homosexuality is destroying moral values and redefining God's original intent and purpose of the family structure. Struggle is seen as a weakness instead of building character. Poverty has become an acceptable way of life for too many with no plan. Success now brings separation, jealousy, and envy within our own race. Love is now diluted with tolerance. Life has little value anymore. The church, while being a beacon of hope and courage, has become afraid itself of the challenge and sacrifice attached to speaking out. Religion, like Humpty-Dumpty, has fallen and shattered into many pieces, beliefs, and gods. Instead of being put back together again, it has reformed each piece as a new, acceptable, and separate entity, absent a unified Savior. We are now at a point where our situation changes us instead of us changing our situation.

Where we go from here depends on from where we came.

Chapter 27

You Can't Slip

In July 2007, a special guest came to talk to the men of our church, Oak Cliff Bible Fellowship—Dr. Tony Evans. Sometimes it takes two Tonys. Tony Dungy is man well known to many in the world of sports—football, to be exact. Tony Dungy is the retired coach of the Indianapolis Colts and Tampa Bay Buccaneers and now is an announcer. I shared the following story in a giveaway booklet I wrote a few years ago, but it bears repeating here.

Tony Dungy is not only a champion in his profession but a champion as a coach, father, and husband and a champion among men. He's also an unwavering, unashamed Christian.

I want to share something he said that gave me pause to think critically. During his talk with the men of the church, which I'm sure closely mimicked a talk with the team, he told of a situation during a game when he was the coach of the Tampa Bay Buccaneers. The game was tight, and every play was crucial. It was third down. A play was called, where his running back was handed the ball, and during the run, there was an opening that could have meant a touchdown, had he made it to the outside lane.

But he didn't make it because he slipped. The field was wet and not in the best shape, but whatever the reason, cutting to make it to the spot caused the runner to slip. The running back went to the sidelines and wasn't in the next play. He stood next to Coach Dungy, who asked him what had happened. The player said, "Coach, I slipped." The field had been beaten up for obvious reasons, he lost his traction, and he slipped.

Coach Dungy looked at him and responded, probably in his calm demeanor, "You can't slip."

When I heard that, I thought, *Man, that's cold!*

This was an example of Tony Dungy's expanded thinking. Coach Dungy explained himself, and then my expanded light came on, and I understood clearly what he meant as he explained to the running back that if he needed longer cleats or gloves or whatever, he should get them, but he couldn't slip.

Here's what I gathered from that: Planning is worth all the effort and time in the world. It's like practice. When you're up against the giants of this world, you have to prepare for whatever obstacles that you might face. Know your environment, and if there is something you can do to avoid a disaster, it is your responsibility to get it done. It is not a mistake if you fail to plan. You can't slip!

Unfortunately, we've all slipped at one time or another. Many of us feel that if we could do it all over again—if perhaps we could have had the knowledge back then—we could have saved ourselves some embarrassing moments in life. We could have saved ourselves a trip to the coach with news he did not want to hear. We would have less to confess—had we only heeded the advice of our trusted friends or listened to the life lessons our grandparents gave us; had we just sat still in church and listened with open minds or not allowed our emotions to take us places we would never have gone, with people we should have never trusted.

But we slipped. Those opportune moments in life only come once, never to return again. What you may see as being a second chance in your life was really a new chance. There really are no such things as second chances but new opportunities to hold your ground, hold your head up high, and not slip. God is a God of new beginnings. He doesn't revisit your bad times. He gives you new chances.

Most of us remember the poem called "Footprints in the Sand," written by an unknown author. It is a small, wonderful, comforting, and thought-provoking piece of work that has been read by literally millions of people. This poem suggests to us that when we look back on our most troubling times in life and wonder, as the old folks would say, "how we got over" or through them, what we see is one set of footprints deeply pressed down into the sands of life, which convinces us that not only was God with us, but He carried us.

But the question that begs an answer is that with each step that He carried you out of harm's way, where did He take you? More importantly, what did you learn from that journey after being carried by your Creator, by the Creator of life itself? Surely, He left more of an impression on you than a footprint in the sand. Did He not leave an impression on your heart? Did He talk with you along the way, filling each step with knowledge and wisdom and truth about your specific life experiences for you to share with others? Did He share with you bits of wisdom to help you through the perils of life?

Or are you still standing in the very spot where He put you down, waiting to hitch another ride? There will come a time in all of our lives when God will not pick us up again. We will not get carried. Some call it destiny. Some call it fate. Others call it death, but what dies? We must all ask ourselves, when we leave this earth, what footprint will we leave? The last footprint left will be named *legacy*.

As I've mentioned, I inherited from my mom her need and dependency on the Lord. Though I am weak and sinfully human, she showed me what true love and sacrifice is. Once you know what it is, you crave it in your life and need to share it. You realize your imperfections but never let them stop you. Watching my mom showed me that failures and tests in life are not done so God can see how bad you are but to show you where you are. My mom was proof that you'll never see what you don't look for, and you'll never question what you don't see as God tries to get your attention.

Everybody has a purpose, but every purpose is only as good as another purpose and is guided by it—a goal. I am a part of a legacy of faith, prayer, and praise to the one and only true God. May my legacy continue through my seed in the name of Jesus.

What legacy will you leave behind that will show the weight, the impression, the footprint of what or who you carried through life? Remember that the deeper the footprint, the heavier the load. How deep will your last footprint be?

Make a difference. Size doesn't matter. No one has to know but God.

Chapter 28

Stay Childlike and Humble

You should never consider yourself as fully grown because you can never grow if you're already fully grown. We are in a perpetual state of growth until death. Never close the door on learning or turn your ear from listening, and never talk too much. Never think too highly or too low of yourself.

When someone pats you on the back for a good you've done, don't turn around too quickly because that open-handed pat on the back will soon turn into a closed-fist punch in the gut. Instead of giving you the benefit of the doubt, others will doubt your benefits. You've worked hard for what you have and what you've become, but live not for what you've become but for what you're becoming. You're still growing. Your plans are not always God's plans. Remember Paul's note to Timothy in the Bible:

> I thank Christ Jesus our Lord, who has given me strength to do his work. He considered me trustworthy and appointed me to serve him, even though I used to blaspheme the name of Christ. In my insolence, I persecuted his people. But God had mercy on me because I did it in ignorance and unbelief. Oh, how generous and gracious our Lord

> was! He filled me with the faith and love that come
> from Christ Jesus. (1 Timothy 1:12–14)

God is looking for people with guts—not cockiness or selfish pride but guts! He's looking for people who are bold enough to not care what other people say, think, or do but are focused on what they think should be done.

Paul was focused on the killing of Christians, regardless of what anyone thought. God felt that if He had those kinds of people with that kind of conviction, they could do great things for the body of Christ, so He chose Paul because Paul had guts!

God's probably not expecting you to walk around with a Bible strapped to each hip, shouting, "Repent, repent!" He wants you to be quiet of spirit and strong of soul, confident of truth, and content of heart, all covered up with a heavy sprinkling of the powdered sugar of joy—unreachable joy.

Old, Feeble, Replaced, and Useless and Irreparable

> Soon your life will snap like a silver chain [growing
> old] or break like a golden bowl [weak and feeble].
> You will be like a broken pitcher at a spring
> [replaced], or broken wheel at a well [useless and
> irreparable]. (Ecclesiastes 12:6)

Take a hard look at your remaining years. It's about time you came to terms with your future. If that doesn't grab you, consider your family in the next decade. What's important to you for them? Have fun, have patience, and have a serious talk with yourself, but not so serious that you can't laugh at yourself or forgive yourself or forgive others.

Respect—it ain't about you!

"Have it your way."

"Do yourself a favor."

"You owe it to yourself."

"You deserve a break today."

Seeing things merely from a human point of view and not from God's perspective can be dangerous. Yet we are all susceptible.

> Because of the privilege and authority God has given me, I give each of you this warning: Don't think you are better than you really are. Be honest in your evaluation of yourselves, measuring yourselves by the faith God has given us. (Romans 12:3)

Keep growing.

Chapter 29

Living Life Abundantly with Disappointments

Peter said that he loved Jesus and was willing to follow Him and to die for Him. I believe that Peter truly believed that. But self-preservation and a little thing called the fear of dying got in the way of living. Peter went through this. We all do—or will, in one way or another. The love that we should have for ourselves we seek from others. The problem with that is that we often overcompensate and allow our eyes to roll back into our heads until all we can see is ourselves and what *we* want—and we lose sight of others. Kinda like not being able to see the forest for the trees because you're standing too close to a tree.

It is said that we should let go of the steering wheel and let God have it whenever we lose control. Well, if your brakes go out, do you let go of the steering wheel? Do you want God to handle the brakes or the steering wheel? No, you fight for your life, not to take over but to guide yourself and maintain control until the Lord brings you to a stop. You don't "Let go and let God," as the saying goes. You do like Jacob did (Genesis 32:22–31): you fight, hold on, and tell that angel that you're not going to let go until he blesses you—vs.28 "because you have struggled with God and with humans and have overcome."

You won't always feel that you have overcome, so what then? What will you do when your hopes and dreams are delayed, expectations fade, or outcomes are unfulfilled past *your* timeline? My work, my marriage, my friends, my plans, my anticipated reciprocal responses—all are disappointing. Did I expect too much? Do I blame myself? Do I blame God? Should I just settle? Do I keep on trying? Can I handle another disappointment?

Life is driven by Purpose. A purpose gives you a drive to keep on moving forward. Longevity, confidence and a will to reach your purpose becomes your goal. We humans yearn for a purpose – 'My purpose' - and we need and search for direction. The Drive is always there searching for the Purpose. Many never discover their purpose but it's not that we all don't have a purpose, it's just that oftentimes we're not actively seeking for that purpose. Life sometime gets in the way and time flies by. We can then feel disappointed in ourselves for not achieving our goals. Our perfect plan didn't work out the way we planned it. God is perfect so we often measure ourselves by perfection. Now What!

Instead of measuring ourselves from the level of perfection, we must measure ourselves from the level of sin. The only way from there is up. We can never start at the level of perfection in our present state of humanity, though we strive for it. But we can always believe.

Sometimes, all we have is all we need. There will be more wrong in this world than right. If life gives you more wrong than right, then it's going to require more forgiveness for wrong than happiness for right. Always be prepared to forgive. Then forget. Then move on.

Life isn't about waiting for the storm to pass; it's about learning how to dance in the rain. Why are we attempting to live a safe life with few mistakes when we could be living a full and abundant life with many mistakes? I'm referring to honest efforts and goals that missed the target. Are we so afraid to step out of our box?

Life is complex. There are no right or wrong answers, it seems, anymore. Some grab life and run with it without borders, and some simply meander through it with no particular goal. Everyone else stands back and judges you on it. Some say that life does not come with an instruction book. Others beg to differ and turn you toward the Bible. Ultimately, I'm afraid the buck stops with you in the form of choices made.

No matter who you are or what choice you make, there will always be someone who lived life before you did, went through what you're going through, and fared much worse or much better. Everyone has a story to tell. Unfortunately, not many will listen and heed the voices of those gone before us. Allow me to offer ten quick perspectives:

1. How we live our lives matters! We are products shaped by our pasts, living in the present, and fighting for our future. Throughout that journey, we sometimes fail to ask ourselves these three questions:
   - What exactly am I looking for in life?
   - Would I know if I found it?
   - Am I whole enough to receive it?
2. "We are not really looking for the meaning of life. We are looking for the experiences of Living."—Bill Moyers
3. We must learn—and teach others—that it doesn't always matter what we expect from life but rather what life expects from us. Something in the future is expecting us. Who or what will we let cut in front of us to stop our progress?
4. What we do is not who we are, but what we did is who we were. We change daily.
5. We live in time (history). God lives in eternity. Thousands of people are born and die in between each blink of God's eye. What a friend we have in Jesus.
6. Let's keep in mind that the things in life—money, homes, riches, spouses—are only keys that unlock doors to happiness and not the keys to life (joy). They are the things that allow us to live a good life, not the things that give us life.

7. Some people are wise for the moment, but a fool is forever. They will fight to gain the world and surrender their souls—a familiar statement indeed.

8. Aging—growing old—is a privilege. Embrace it.

9. We live in spectrums of time. Some people, places, and things in our lives are seasonal. They are there for just that moment in time and not forever. I believe that is the will of God on purpose. It is up to us to learn from, accept, and take joy in each season God gives us.

10. "He, God, knows your end at your beginning, and no matter how much you 'mess up,' you will never lose your position."—Yolanda Adams

Chapter 30

Always Remember
to Never Forget

Never forget *who*

- Loves you
- Helped you
- Made you cry
- Made you laugh
- Prayed for you
- Made your life better
- Made your life worse

Never forget *what*

- Made you cry
- Made you go down on your knees to pray
- Made your life simpler
- Made your life worse
- Was said to you
- Was done to you
- Was done for you

Never forget *when* you

- Laughed the hardest
- Cried the most
- Were the happiest
- Were the saddest
- Knew that he or she was the one for you

Never forget *where*

- You were when you heard the good news
- You were when you got the bad news
- To go for help
- To go when you just need to get away
- Your heart is

Never forget *why* you

- Were born
- Are so blessed
- Do what you do for a living
- Got married
- Decided not to get married again

Chapter 31

Serve or Be Served

That is the question. Man was created by God with the need to be needed, to be physically and emotionally touched. Woven into that need is a seed called stress—stress to conform, stress to perform, stress to prove love. Stress is the result of pressure. If stress can burst a steel pipe, just imagine what it can do to the human body or the human psyche—the human soul and mind. We must take care of what's important to us, each other, and one another. We must learn to serve and not focus on being served. That's not something we were born with.

We were born with an inherited, childlike, selfish, and sinful nature that must be trained and taught to care, share, and serve as a way of life. It must be trained to see the importance of that, to embrace it, and to see and accept that we have this selfish nature within us, kicking and screaming to be served. We have been taught to grab and hold on to instead of sharing and conforming to the comfort of others. We must learn to say before a funeral what we say at the funeral.

We must understand the art of forgiveness and how to live with our weakness to forget. One of the main purposes of telling people that you love them is to allow people to know it so that they won't have to go through so much to show it. This chapter should not take ten to twenty pages for you to understand the point that I'm trying to make here. Sit down alone one day and take an honest evaluation of yourself through the eyes of others. It doesn't mean you have to stress yourself out with feelings of guilt or tell everyone you know that you're sorry—though there may be some people in your life who need to hear that, and that should be expressed with honesty. Otherwise, *I'm sorry* is just an excuse for bad behavior. Change your behavior. Sometimes that's more important than words. *I love you* and *I'm sorry* come from the same family of hesitancy.

Acceptance is the water that puts out the fire. The smoldering smoke may take some time, but it soon rises and dissipates, then disappears. The smell may be a constant reminder to you of what happened in the past or remind you of the pain, but memories are always in your past, not your future.

Learn to forgive yourself, and, as the Bible says, ask for forgiveness for the "guilt" of your sins because upon acceptance, your sins have already been paid for and forgiven. Lean on Jesus, but know that you're not Jesus. You make mistakes.

Chapter 32

Liquid Words: Under the Influence of Emotions

Why is weeping seen as a sign of weakness? We cry when we are hurt and saddened. We cry when we are overjoyed and happy. We cry when we are moved with pain or pity.

I once had a personal talk with a favorite pastor of mine about a personal situation that I was going through, and he told me that I had a "sensitive soul." I cried.

If you feel your lowest, would not the one you love the most be the one you want to weep in front of? The one who loves you the most? Jesus wept in front of His Father! Then He died and rose from the dead. It takes more courage to cry than to laugh, and even more strength to cry in front of those who see you as strong. Tears are liquid words, deep within the heart and soul. It's a language that only those who truly love you can understand or translate.

Instead of speaking in tongues, you're speaking in tears. Tears flow from what are considered the windows of your soul. Tears deserve your utmost attention and empathy, not shame or fear. To be ashamed to cry is to be ashamed to hurt, or show joy, or show love.

Stop crying "past" tears, and start crying "future" tears, not about what happened but about what's going to happen. Stop crying tears of pain, and start crying tears of deliverance, not about who or what hurt you but how much better the hurt will strengthen you and your bond. As much as there is a God who wants to help you, there is a devil who wants to hurt you. I'm not saying not to acknowledge your part in that hurt or pain but to understand the root of the pain and hurt.

Sometimes, the hardest person to forgive is yourself. We all have a weakness, a point where envy and anger can enter and cause us to do or say things that cause hurt and pain to others. But again I say, we are human, not Jesus. We are and should be viewed by the standard of sin, not of perfection, while striving for better. That road to perfection will be paved with tears—tears of pain and heartbreak, tears of disappointment and disagreement, tears of confusion and lack of direction, and tears of loneliness and abandonment. But the closer you get to your destination, those tears that emanate from the same point of origin—the heart—turn into tears of gratitude, grace, appreciation, love, thankfulness, release from bondage, and freedom. You just have to *believe*!

If no one is there to pick you up, pick yourself up. Sometimes all you have is all you need. You know others love you when they forgive you, even when you don't deserve it. Like Jesus did for you. He sees you at your worst, and He forgives you. He listens to your mouth, but He hears your heart and speaks to your tears. You confess it, and He forgives you. It doesn't have to be so complicated.

Sometimes troubles can be so deep within you that no one can see them. No one can know that is why you said what you said or did what you did that hurt you so. You can scream at such a high pitch for help that no one can hear it. How, indeed, can one who is drowning ask for help with a mouth full of water? What will you do in the face of someone else's pain? Will you run, or will you help? Will you ask God why, or will you ask yourself, *Why me?*

Tears can be a cry for help. People need a reason to live. Like it or not, we are our brother's keeper. We are many people's reason for living, and we must take that responsibility seriously.

Cry your heart out with pride, and let go of that burden, and somehow, move on. Love the one who is willing to listen and wipe away your tears.

Chapter 33

Dealing with Conflict

Hate and love come from the same source within us. Your reaction to each one is the same and can be extreme and overwhelming. Each requires much thought and much control. In this chapter are statements of the need to resolve our differences, control our emotions, and simply make better decisions in the midst of confrontation. Conflict requires mediation. Sometimes we need meditation and thought before the event, in anticipation of it.

Avoiding conflict involves knowing yourself, your propensities, your hot buttons, and your limits. Conflict always involves someone else, although sometimes there are conflicts within us that are far greater than the conflicts outside of us. Conflict is about power and fear. Conquer both, and you can conquer conflict. Always remember: don't get upset, get angry. Getting upset affects you. Getting angry affects your target.

Is resolving conflict a matter of behavior or attitude? Let's first define both. *Behavior* is defined as the way in which one acts or conducts oneself, especially toward others; it's how one acts in response to a particular situation or stimulus. *Attitude* is defined as a certain way of thinking or feeling about someone or something, typically one that is reflected in a person's behavior. It may be bias that is based on behavior.

The objective is to change the results of conflict, to change the way in which you act or think. One side says that if you change your attitude, it will change how others view your behavior. The other side says that you must first change your behavior in order to change others' attitudes about you. But who or what determines the standard for behavior? Whatever you do, how you react to certain situations will reflect on who you are. Your behavior will determine how others see you, and they will project that view on those who are like you.

Your reaction to certain situations must be carefully thought out because it just doesn't affect you but is a reflection on those who are like you. That formulates an opinion of bias against you and others that may not be correct. That is not meant to put the blame on your shoulders; it is simply that bias is an uncontrollable virus that causes conflict.

Here are ten quotes, notes, and suggestions on conflict that should be discussed and considered:

1. "Hell hath no fury like a woman scorned," except a man deceived (Proverbs 6:34–35 (paraphrased translation). There are always two sides to every conflict, and one side is usually left out of the conversation. Consider both.
2. Better is open rebuke than love that is concealed (Proverbs 25:5). This basically says that it's better to get it out than to suppress anger, while maintaining control.
3. Rise above your conflict, and vow to never cry alone again.
4. Conflict has to do with fear and power. Fear is simply power as seen through the eyes, with its hands raised in defeat. Fear and power cannot cohabitate in the same place at the same time. One has to give in to the other for the other to move forward.
5. Former president Bill Clinton once said, "People have always been more impressed by the power of our example than by

the example of our power." This seems to say that we must be stronger in character than in conflict.

6. We do too much of two things: we give the devil too much credit, and we don't take responsibility for our own actions.

7. Pastor and educator Voddie Baucham has said, "Jealousy is the sin of not being satisfied with what God has given you." Sometimes the conflict is from within.

8. I make mistakes. Don't look at my humanity—it is flawed— but look at what I believe in my heart. Then forgive me. Then, forgive me again.

9. Stress breeds conflict. It's important to release it in order to make room for more. Pressure can burst a pipe. Think of what it can do to you.

10. Conflict of the conundrum: If I do what I know is wrong, while I may be better off, I'm no better than they are. I then become what I hate—I become one of them.

Chapter 34

Dealing with Pain, Change, and Loss

The American musical phenomenon known as Frankie Beverly & Maze said it this way: "Joy and pain are like sunshine and rain." The Bible says that when it rains, it rains on both the just and the unjust, just as the sun shines on both as well.

What are you willing to give up for peace? Pain and loss are by-products of love. If you squeeze love long and hard enough, it becomes painful. If you squeeze pain long and hard enough, you'll start to accept it and fall in love with it. Expressing your true feelings exposes your humanity. One of the marks of spiritual maturity is the quiet confidence that God is in control, without the need to understand why He does what He does (Daniel 4:35). This chapter expresses the thoughts and voices of those who just want to walk with you:

1. *Hurt* is when you expected something you didn't receive. That's expectation. *Happy* is when you get something you didn't expect. That's expectancy. *Joy* is when you can get hurt and still be happy. Learn to count it all as joy.

2. Sometimes, things simply change. We don't like change, but we must be willing to give up the life we planned in order to make way for the life God has planned for us.

3. The reality is that death is a part of God's plan—the clay pot is in the hands of the Potter.

4. "Character cannot be developed in ease and quiet. Only through the experiences of trial and suffering can the soul be strengthened, vision cleared, ambition inspired and success achieved."—Helen Keller

5. "Because of a critical time in my life, I lost my direction and did not trust my own stability, so 'I walked close to the wall'"—Jane Fonda

6. "No need to be ashamed of tears, for tears bore witness that a man [humankind] has the greatest courage, the courage to suffer."—Viktor Frankl

7. We live in a tough world, and we have to be tougher than it to overcome it, or it will consume us. Alone, we will be destroyed, unless God sustains us, for true growth happens not when you gain something but when you lose something.

8. Help often comes disguised as cruelty.

9. Change requires a lot to unlearn. It requires letting go of the past that was given to you and accepting the present to allow you a guilt-free future.

10. Pain and loss are sometimes only the change of seasons in one's life. We must accept the things we cannot change and not stand still or move backward. We must move forward with courage and love and life. Some problems aren't complicated; they're just painful.

Chapter 35

Inspiration

Inspiration is the cheerleader for hope. It clarifies your needs versus your wants. It points you toward education and excellence and defines your reason for struggle and risk-taking. Its spellbinding smell draws others to support and believe in you. It puts skin on your words, gives sight to your visions of grandeur, and the courage to stretch out your hands to reach your seemingly unobtainable goals. A fall is just a stumble for which nothing or no one braces you. But be careful of how you treat people because the very thing that allows you to get up from your fall may be the very thing—or person—you've been walking on all along. Let's be inspired by the inspirational voices of others:

1. As much as you believe in yourself, you need someone to believe in you. When someone you respect validates you, that means everything, if not the difference between success and failure. Choose your mentors wisely.

2. When we are driven, *why* we do something almost always controls *what* we do in our lives. That will determine when we do it. The *who* is up to us, and the *where* doesn't matter. The *how* becomes the task at hand.

3. He who has a *why* to live for can bear with almost any *how*.—Friedrich Nietzsche

4. A person who becomes conscious of the responsibility he bears toward a human being will never be able to throw away his life or take his own or destroy another's.

5. To say that "God is good" says that I'm still hurting, but I'm still standing, though your help may be needed.

6. Some people may say that you think that you are better than they are. If you are worthy of that comment, then don't back down. But if you don't back down to it, you'd better humbly live up to it.

7. I'm not afraid of your voodoo. I don't throw salt over my shoulder. I don't need to cross my fingers. I don't need to knock on wood. I don't need to cut the foot off a defenseless rabbit. I'll set up a tent under a ladder, and I'll chase a black cat down and dare him to cross my line. I now live by faith.

8. No one's perfect, but then, Christ didn't die for perfect people. Where does that put you?

9. To be successful, you will be disappointed many times. But if you don't expect much, you'll never be disappointed.

10. You can't be all things to all people. You can only be yourself, and somebody's gonna want that.—Robert Gion

Chapter 36

Motivation

Motivation is a Greek word with Latin roots that means "to move." Does motivation come from you or from others? The job of a motivator is to move you toward that desire, thought, drive, willingness, or passion needed to wake up the sleeping giant in you, convincing you to take the necessary steps toward achieving a specific goal.

Is your goal to simply make it or to exceed your goal? Is failure an option or an obstacle? How do you respond to difficult situations along the way to your goal? Do you expect to change yourself or to change the world? This chapter offers the words of motivators whose desires were stronger than their fears. Some are thoughts for you to ponder, but don't ponder too long because motivators move! So say you, voices:

1. When asked what his motivation for success is, Howard Schultz, of Starbucks fame, replied, "You cannot exceed the expectations of your customers until you exceed the expectations of your employees."
2. People respond well to people who are sure of what they want.—Anna Wintour
3. Life will be very difficult at times, but the unique opportunity lies in the way in which you bear your burdens.

4. Forces beyond your control can take away everything you possess except one thing: your freedom to choose how you will respond to the situation. You cannot always control what happens to you in life, but you can always control what you will do about what happens to you.—Victor Frankl

5. People who change the world take chances.

6. Whenever it seems that God has turned His back on you, it only means that He is turning around, not to leave you but asking you to follow Him. Perhaps you're going the wrong way.

7. When we get to a point in our lives when we are no longer able to change our situations, we must then change ourselves.

8. Great people achieve great things by doing things they love to do. Don't stop looking. Find it and occupy it, and don't settle.

9. "God only hits a moving target and He can hit that target with a crooked stick."—(Dr. Tony Evans) All you need to do is trust Him.

10. "How you think is gonna either lift you up or trip you up."—Reverend Charles Stanley

Chapter 37

In Spirit

What is your biggest spiritual problem? What is your deepest prayer? Does God agree with you? Is faith simply motivation or reality to you? Who is Jesus to you? Does sin hinder God's purpose for you? Is the church relevant anymore? It doesn't seem to deter evil. Whose job is that anyway? Is wisdom simply a passing thought captured? This introduces us to our Source.

I read a story once titled *Death in Tehran*. I'd like to break bread with you on it:

A rich and mighty Persian walked in his garden with one of his servants. The servant cried out that he had just encountered Death, who had threatened him. He begged his master to give him his fastest horse so that he could make haste and flee to Tehran, which he could reach that same evening. The master consented, and the servant galloped off on the horse.

Upon returning to his house, the master himself met Death and questioned him, "Why did you terrify and threaten my servant?"

"I did not threaten him," said Death. "I only showed surprise in finding him still here when I planned to meet him tonight in Tehran."

Three contemplative thoughts:

- Sometimes it's better to stand and face your fears than run from them. Running *from* them can turn out to be running *to* them.
- Approach your problems with faith, not fear. Fear is simply power with its hands raised in defeat. Don't accept it as your own. The master in that story never approached Death as if Death was looking for him.
- Don't be afraid to question your fear. You may learn something that could prevent you from making it worse, or you could stop it all together. The servant never questioned Death. He just accepted him as fate. The master questioned him.

Now, let's listen to the voices of others:

1. One of our biggest spirit problems is that we don't want to know God. We only want God to know us.
2. We are saved through trust and delivered by faith. God gives us what it takes to be saved—not on our own, but we must accept what is offered from God so that we will be delivered from the Law to grace.
3. You don't lead broken people to Christ—the cross. You take Christ—the cross—to broken people. It is ultimately up to those people to accept the offer.
4. "Before you truly give in to Jesus, you must first give in to yourself; your own mortality, weaknesses, propensities and flawed humanity."—Larry Moyer
5. We are sealed by the Holy Spirit upon acceptance of Christ. If you can't be good enough to get it, you can't be bad enough to lose it. That's grace.—Chuck Swindoll

6. God violates neither His perfection nor man's free will, for to do either fails to accomplish His goal—voluntary obedience.

7. Some believe that church has become like a movie. I leave from my life, enter into a building, drop a few coins in to watch, and be entertained by a two-hour fantasy. When it's over, I leave and go back to my real life. What a shame.

8. Some say that our problem with God is that we've left our first love, but the problem now, generationally, is that they've never loved Him first.

9. Faith is belief in the absence of proof. Faith is a motivator, not a result.

10. Always be content but never satisfied.

Chapter 38

In Conclusion but Never the End

How do we pay attention to the details if we are told "don't sweat the small stuff" when the small stuff is the details? True life is not viewed from far away but close up, where the small details are. When I look up at the stars of creation, they look small, as does the sun, as do the highest mountains and my ability to capture a single view of a vast ocean with one glance. They all look like small stuff from a distance, but up close, they will consume me. Even God is small to us from a distance, yet Moses was allowed to see only God's back as He passed by on Mount Sinai, lest he be consumed.

Common sense is said to be the sense we have in common. It is the incubator for wisdom. It is derived from the proper assembly of day-to-day accumulated data. If common sense is no longer common, it means that people are changing the norms.

> All the people did whatever seemed right in their own eyes. (Judges 21:25)

They basically abandoned common sense.

The one thing we will never be short of in this world is advice. Creation has given us two ears, not only so that we may hear but that we may hear both sides. We have two eyes, not just to see but to see both sides. Our fingers are strategically positioned that when one is pointed, the others point back to us. But to have two eyes and accept what you know is wrong or two ears and believe what you know to be untrue shows little common sense.

Luke 8:18 (KJV) says, "Take heed therefore how ye hear:..." So pay attention to "how" you hear (or listen), not to 'what' you hear. The word *how* speaks to the way or manner in which you heard the Word or information. Was it in passing, secondhand, by eavesdropping? What was the condition or quality of the word you heard? Did you only hear part or all of the word or information? One side or both sides? Was it authenticated? What was your physical or mental state when you heard it?

> Jesus knew the Pharisees had heard that he was baptizing and making more disciples than John (though Jesus himself didn't baptize them—his disciples did). (John 4:1–2)

We have to be able to separate fact from emotions. Understand before you take a stand. A lot could be riding on your words or response.

We put a lot of pressure on ourselves because we are no longer comfortable with contentment, and we scoff at normalcy. Contentment is important, but you can't live there if something is waiting for you in your future. Be content but never satisfied, allowing yourself room to move, should God say to move or should He still have plans for you.

James Baldwin was asked why he moved to and stayed in Istanbul. He said that he needed "a place where I can stop and do nothing in order to start again ... to begin again demands a certain silence, a certain privacy." We all could use a place to simply be still and to think and express without fear or interruption—a place where we can reintroduce ourselves to us, a place where at least there is a reason why no one cares, a place where we are no longer afraid of losing someone but instead can find ourselves, a place where *no one* knows our names.

Take some time for yourself. Take care of yourself. During the January 6 congressional debate on the invasion on the Capitol building in Washington, DC, Senate Majority Leader Mitch McConnell said, "We must not imitate nor escalate what we repudiate." In plain English, we must not do or encourage the things that are detrimental to us. This can also be applied to our individual decisions that we make every day.

"A mind is a terrible thing to waste." This saying is familiar to many, especially our older generation. What a true statement. I read somewhere that the mind is a muscle; it needs to be stretched to stay sharp. It needs to be prodded and pushed and challenged to perform at its peak. If you let it get idle and lazy, then that muscle will become a pitiful mass of flab in a short time.

I have a high-performance car that I do not drive often. When I do drive it, it sputters and is less responsive until I get it out on the highway and open it up to a high (but lawful) speed, which blows out the cobwebs that settled in its fuel injector due to its being idle for so long. After that, it stabilizes itself to a smooth, comfortable, and powerful ride. Such is the idle and unused mind.

Left idle, your mind will accept and believe anything that flows through the portals of the mouth, ears, and eyes. If you don't feed it the truth, it will get fat with bad thoughts, untruths, rumors, and lies and will develop an open-door policy that will be difficult to close. If you watch what you eat, you should also watch what you hear and monitor your thoughts.

Our minds are altered and molded by the results of our actions. If you don't have time, then you're not managing your time wisely, based on what is important to your well-being. Read, travel, and learn.

There is very little Christian representation on everyday television, except for a few hours on Sundays. It should be very concerning that the church no longer represents mainstream Christianity in America, as our older generations tag out to the new generation. We no longer speak the same language so how can we communicate? We no longer share the same dreams so how do we grow? We no longer have the same goals so how do we define success? How? We think and pray and are not afraid to ask for help.

Learn to master the art of listening—more listening, less hearing. Listening takes focus, care, concern, intent, and a caring heart. You may not agree with all that you hear, but you don't hear unless you listen. It takes no effort to hear, but it takes intent to listen. Gather all of the information, emotions, and understanding before you give your two cents.

Don't load your gun while the other person is talking. Be as confident as you can in your response, and don't be afraid to say *I don't know*. Feel the words before you size up the conversation. Consider all alternatives, and sift your conscience through what Jesus would do, even as you know that you are not Jesus. Try to put yourself in the shoes of the person, without owning the shoes.

People are searching to be understood. Know that it's not your problem or concern, that you are there to help with the load but not to carry the load. Once you've helped the little old lady to cross the street, let her go. Don't carry her in your mind for the rest of your journey. Learn to give and let go.

Don't own your words; borrow them from the Lord. Also, as Luke 8:18 says, "So pay attention to how you hear." In what way or manner did you hear the words said? Did you hear all of the story? In what mental states were you and the concerned person?

Advice can be helpful or deadly. Know that Satan is in the details as well, so don't hold yourself hostage to bad advice. Satan then would get two for the price of one.

Lastly, create new dreams—what I call the *dream after the dream*. There is always a next chapter in your life, God willing. Life does not end after your work or career ends. Yes, your career, your job, your life's work will eventually end, but don't let it catch you by surprise. Nothing happens without a plan. As the old saying goes, "People don't plan to fail; they fail to plan."

Multiple streams of income would be a nice comfort factor because, like anything else in this world, there is always a cost. The coronavirus pandemic in 2020 gave people a chance to focus on what is important in their lives. They thought about finances, family, health, and purpose.

Never abandon love, intimacy, marriage, or marriage again; even embrace your singlehood. You are allowed to change, morally speaking. You no longer have to do whatever you habitually did in your adult life. You can change deodorant or cologne or perfume or your haircut or hairstyle or the make of car you drive. You don't have to live where you live or wear what you've always worn. Don't be afraid to be afraid. Life expectancy has changed, and there is no expiration date on living your life, as long as you do it responsibly and in consideration of others. But like anything else that you do successfully, it has to be planned. Nothing just happens.

You must learn how to deal with the psychological and emotional issues of change. It is possible that your best life may be what you do next. In your forties, fifties, sixties, and beyond, you know yourself better. You don't have to work full time; maybe you'll work part-time, maybe do volunteer work, maybe get involved in a personal project based on your prior work experience or something totally different. Write that book you've always wanted to write and give motivational speeches on the experiences that could positively benefit others. People are living longer these days.

But the thing that you need to do while you are younger—in order to benefit from your older years—is first take care of your body. It's the only one you have. Don't let your car or your home look better than that which houses your soul. Also, take an honest review of the important relationships in your life and see where they stack up to your past and future plans. We unfortunately focus on the flaws instead of what made our love and relationships special. Then, don't be afraid to reinvent yourself. Change can be good, but if you are comfortable and confident with where you are, stay polished, and stay sharp.

You can't talk about dreams and goals without talking about patience, risks, and failures. Patience is a mindset, a determination, a decision to accept, rest, succeed, and abide under the pressures of life through endurance. Remember this: there is no failure except that which is first created in your mind—the what-ifs of the world.

God asked that we believe Him, regardless of the risks, in spite of the danger, and ignoring the odds. If you do what He tells you and go where He leads you, the outcome will always be a victory, never a failure. Believe only what you can authenticate.

The Bible has sixty-six books, said to have been written over a 1,500-year period from over forty different people, none of whom we have met. They, however, are validated and authenticated by witnesses who were there, so we believe their written documents as proof, as we do in today's courts of law. None of us has personally met those who have shaped our lives and laws from years past— Martin Luther King Jr., Frederick Douglas, George Washington. Did Christopher Columbus really sail the seven seas? An undocumented statement that I heard on a television program interview from the late Charlie Daniels said: 'I don't believe two rocks crashed together, fell into the ocean, we crawled out, climbed up a tree, fell down, broke our tails off, and went to Harvard.' Who created the rocks that crashed together, or the rock it fell on, the ocean it fell in, or the tree we climbed up, the gravity that snatched us down from our perch, or the knowledge and ability to be educated? What about rain, the sun, the moon, the wind, and oxygen?

Every building has a builder, every painting has a painter, every meal has a cook, and every child has parents. There are too many unanswered questions and no witnesses. The search for black-and-white answers dulls the open mind and destroys the thinking process. It shrinks possibilities down to the simplest acceptable form. As we get older, we began to question our understanding, and we realize more and more that life isn't as black and white as we once saw it. The more we see of the world—through travel and technology and books—the more it complicates what was once simple and acceptable. We search for satisfaction, not answers. A narrow doorway will not only accept only so much but will deny even more. Perhaps you missed the mark because you aimed low.

Get in touch or stay in touch with your moral center. Success without morals is a disaster waiting to happen and will be unrewarded. Don't just leave future generations a financial will; leave a moral will as well. Be nice, but don't be used.

Life is so short. We don't have many years or much time. Are you concerned about who will advise your child, our youth, when you're gone? Does it seem like the world is moving and changing faster, and you won't have time to say all that you'd like to say before your children are grown and gone and disappear into the fog of this world that pulls on them in every direction, without their having all of the information needed to survive? What position in life will they assume? Will they become beggars or givers? Are they mature enough to seek God's help? All they will have to lean on are the conversations about life that you had with them, especially as a single parent.

In Get Up! God's Children Don't Beg, D. Steve Walker illuminates common failures in the struggle to build a stable foundation for making sense of life, racial issues, and the absence of a happy life. The main culprit is the lack of common information and when and how to communicate it. D. Steve Walker examines the importance of relationships, facing your fears, the "positive" effects of white privilege, and what Black Lives Matter should really mean for everyone involved and why. This book talks about:

- How to deal with personal conflict in your life and how to manage it to avoid self destruction
- What it means to live an abundant life with disappointments
- The importance of rest

D. Steve Walker shows how we must change our thinking in order to change our lives. He's convinced that you can do so. We all can. All we need is information and a willingness to slow down, understand before we take a stand, and then to assume the position of control and not chaos. You can do this. Yes, you can!

Printed in the United States
by Baker & Taylor Publisher Services